Life Around my Father
Harry Edwards

by Felicity Joan Medland

Phyllis Dorothy White (1898-1969) who had kept up a correspondence with Dad throughout the First World War while he was on active service. They were married in April 1922. Throughout the Balham years she supported him in his political career and later when they opened our home to become the Balham Psychic Research Society. She gave Dad all the support he needed on their journey which would eventually bring us all to Burrows Lea. Her devotion and loyalty to Dad was recognised by all who knew them. My sisters and I still miss her dearly.

Life Around my Father
Harry Edwards

by Felicity Joan Medland

Published by
Burrows Lea Country House Limited

Published by:
Burrows Lea Country House Limited
Burrows Lea
Hook Lane, Shere
Guildford, GU5 9QG, UK
2008

Telephone: 01483 202054
E-mail: healing@burrowslea.org.uk
www.sanctuary-burrowslea.org.uk

Typesetting: John Medland
Cover design: Matthew Power
Proofreader: Helen Beck

ISBN 978-1-904149-13-8

Printed by the West Island Group Limited
Afton Road, Freshwater, Isle of Wight. PO40 9TT

Dedication

*This book is dedicated to the furtherance of Burrows Lea and
to all those who continue with the work that Dad started*

ACKNOWLEDGMENTS

Here is the authentic account of the rise of our founder, Harry Edwards, to become the wonderful and inspiring spiritual healer that he was.

It is written by his eldest daughter, Felicity, who together with her two sisters, Megan and Barbara and his grandchildren, are the true link to that great spiritual healer. Unacknowledged until now, they are in our midst and carry the message that Harry Edwards is with us still.

Paul White, Chairman of Harry Edwards Healing Sanctuary Limited

January 2008

Many thanks to my cousin Alan Pool for the help he has given me in editing this book. F.J.M.

INTRODUCTION

This is a book of recollections of the life and times of Henry James Edwards (1893-1976), by his eldest daughter Felicity Joan Medland. It concentrates on the middle years of the life of "Harry" Edwards, the founder of the spiritual healing sanctuary at Burrows Lea. He was instrumental in establishing The National Federation of Spiritual Healers and became the most famous spiritual healer of the Twentieth Century.

The book is not a biography or an explanation of the theory of spiritual healing. There are many other publications dealing with those subjects. This is a personal testimony illustrating the personality of the man and his domestic surroundings in the years when he became aware of his destiny and began to develop his outstanding gift.

Felicity Medland shows how a hidden hand of destiny seemed to lead her father from one prepared stage to the next, in war, marriage, business and politics to his intimate friendship with the extraordinary physical medium Jack Webber. After this brief interlude Harry Edwards was convinced of the potential power of the spirit and wrote his first book, *The Mediumship of Jack Webber*.

The narrative provides a close insight into the lives of the printer-politician and his family in the difficult years of the Great Depression. To the struggle of sustaining a solvent business and raising a family were added the pressures of political activism and the organisation of the new spiritualist work.

The Second World War added the strains of evacuation, rationing and the additional workload of service in the Home Guard for Harry Edwards and his wife Phyllis who became an ARP warden. Despite finding their home on the front line of the German Blitz, Harry still found time to make long journeys across blacked-out London to address public meetings and to visit the sick and the dying.

At the end of the war the family were obliged to leave their bomb-wrecked home and Harry gave his printing business to his brother Ernie and took a leap into the unknown. He became a full time spiritual healer, completely dependent on voluntary donations sent through the post.

The latter part of the book records the founding of the healing sanctuary at Burrows Lea near the village of Shere in Surrey, and the three decades of Harry Edward's national and global fame as he assisted millions of sufferers both directly and through "absent healing".

In the final part of the book, after Harry Edward's death, we are reminded of how his work continues and that the power to heal that he demonstrated in abundance remains available for all those who wish for it.

Harry Edwards photographed on active duty in the First World War.
Unusually he was commissioned in the field and rose to the rank of Captain.

CONTENTS

This is my father's drawing of Lloyd George found in the autograph book his sisters gave him to take to India in 1915.

Lloyd George knew my father

"If ever you wrote a book about your father, what would you use as a title?" asked my friend, Mary Hammond. I had the answer, "Lloyd George knew my Father" (which he did) "Oh Fel, you can't choose that" said Mary, who was not a Liberal supporter. This left me a bit torn, between my father's great admiration for the Prime Minister, who had fired his enthusiasm for the Liberal cause, and Mary's opinion, which I had always valued. But as the writing progressed, it became apparent that this was the story of life around my father Harry Edwards.

Lloyd George knew my father
Father knew Lloyd George

These two lines, sung repeatedly to the tune of *Onward, Christian Soldiers* was something to fall back on during wartime route marches after we had 'rolled out the barrel', 'hung out the washing on the Siegfried Line', and met someone improperly dressed 'coming round the mountain'. However those lines did have some meaning for me as my father, during his political career in the 1920s and 1930s, was brought into contact on more than one occasion with the great Lloyd George, the last Liberal Prime Minister, who had led this nation to victory during the First World War and gave us the Old Age Pension.

So if I am to write anything, it will be how life was, and how it circulated around the man who was to emerge from being a printer and a politician to become the greatest Spiritual Healer of the Twentieth Century. In the 1920s and early thirties, Dad was a printer and a politician and the words 'spiritual healer' had never entered his thoughts. He, like so many others, was struggling to get through the years of the Great Depression, trying to keep a business running and a family fed.

Looking back now on that time between the two World Wars is like looking back on the pages of history. I find I have a yearning for those years when the world I grew up in was a much more gentle and relaxed place, where words like calories, allergies, stress, cot deaths, psycho this and psycho that, either did not exist, or were lying undiscovered in dictionaries. Life, though very hard for some was much simpler, social standards were high and childhood went on a lot longer. From those days in Balham to Burrows Lea, the now well known Healing Sanctuary at Shere, so many events were to take place in my father's life before he became the well known healer, and a man of such great character. Burrows Lea lay many years ahead but life had to be lived throughout the years that revolved around us during the 1920s and the 1930s. They were to lead us as a family and our Dad on a journey through the time of the Great Depression and then through the years of the Second World War. The county of Surrey was waiting for us when peace was ours at last. We made the move to Stoneleigh then on to Burrows Lea. This is the story of how life was lived around my father during those earlier years.

If ever there were a life destined to run with a well-designed blueprint, it was the life of my father. There were so many set stages, each one leading on to the next, which brought a small-time printer to walk on to the largest platforms in this country and abroad to demonstrate the power of Spiritual Healing. This story started on the 29th May 1893 when Dad was born north of the Thames in London at 79 Crayford Road, Upper Holloway, to Henry James Edwards and Emma Jane (née Buist).

He was the first of their nine children. After two years in Upper Holloway, followed by ten in Wood Green, they moved south of the river, first to Vauxhall and then to 13 Shipka Road in Balham, South West London, not long before the war with Germany - to become known as the First World War - was declared in 1914 on the first of August.

This was to change Dad's life. He was 21 and had followed his father, Henry James Edwards, into the printing trade but put that behind him to serve his country and enlisted in the Royal Sussex Regiment. It was not, however, his destiny to spend the war, as so many did, on the battlefields of France. Towards the end of 1915 he embarked on the *SS Ceramic* for service, first in India, where he was transferred to the King George's Own Sappers and Miners, and then with the Mesopotamia Expeditionary Force in Baghdad. Whilst based in Baghdad, he was promoted by Lt Gen Sir William Raine Marshall from corporal to Second Lieutenant and became involved in laying a railway from Baghdad to Tikrit, and in the construction of bridges for carrying military vehicles in North West Persia, drawing on local labour as he moved through the country. He returned home from Baghdad in 1921.

Both my mother's family and my father's lived near to each other in Balham, and had known each other well before the first world war began. But when war broke out my mother, Phyllis White, and her family moved to Long Bredy in Dorset where my grandfather became farm bailiff for the Kingston Russell estate. It was from Long Bredy during those long years of war that Mum kept up a correspondence with Dad. When he returned from Baghdad he proposed to her in Dorchester Museum. They were married in St Mary's Church in Balham on 17th April 1922 and settled down there in a terraced house in Balham at No 11 Childebert Road.

I was born in April 1923, the eldest of four children, and had the fortune to arrive twenty minutes after April Fool's Day for which I was very thankful. My father, being a great tease, would have had a 'field day'. As I grew up it amused him to introduce me to his friends and colleagues as "This is my eldest and ugliest daughter," As it happened this turned out to be true. Tony was born in 1926, to be followed in 1928 by Megan, who was named after Megan Lloyd George, and in 1931 by Barbara.

Dad chose my name, Felicity, for which I never really thanked him. It is a name with which I have never been comfortable. Felicity means happiness, and I must say having a father like mine ensured me plenty of that. I was also given another name. Soon after I was born there was a wretched play on in London called *Bunty Pulls The Strings* and to the whole family, 'Bunty' I became. It always made me feel like something in a stable. I remember Miss Hall, my teacher at Ravenstone School, querying the decision to call me Felicity. She had asked the class to go and find for themselves a poem which expressed great feeling and beauty. "For instance" she said, "you may like to consider the words of Keats.

> *A thing of beauty is a joy for ever.*
> *Its loveliness increases,*
> *Never shall it pass into nothingness.*

We were all to present our 'finds' at the next poetry lesson. I could not wait .When it was my turn to stand up and deliver my words of deep feeling and beauty I was ready to recite:

> *I saw a woman going from place to place,*
> *Searching for her child's face.*
> *I heard her crying, crying, crying.*
> *And in a flash saw the sea trying*
> *With savage joy and efforts wild,*
> *To smash its rocks with a dead child.*

Outside No 11 Childebert Road. Ethel Edwards , my Mum, me and a dog called Don

The wedding on the 17th April 1922.
Mum and dad with the bridesmaids Marjorie White, Marjorie Edwards and Lily Edwards.

This is Childebert Road and how it looked in 1939. During the second world war all of the iron railings and gates were
removed for the manufacture of war weapons. As the privet hedges were no longer restrained by the railings, they also went.
No's 1,3 5,7 & 9 were destroyed by bombs.

"Well, it is not exactly what I had in mind," said Miss Hall, and as an afterthought continued "I wonder how the name of Felicity came to be chosen for you".

Setting up a business between the two wars presented many difficulties: as times were hard and money was very scarce. However, after his demobilisation in late 1921, Dad went ahead and leased a shop in nearby Bedford Hill. It was double fronted with a stationers in one half and a printing business the other. The Great Depression, and unemployment that came with it, created the situation where the shop had to be sold. It passed into the hands of a Mr Bird, and the printing plant was moved to a building in the mews at the back of Hildreth Street. "There is nothing more depressing," Dad once said to me "than having a shop full of stock when no one comes in to buy."

The printing business kept us going on a knife edge until the middle of the 1930s when Dad and a Mr Mushens formed a partnership and it was moved again, this time to Balham High Road. They called it "Essential Services". As before, it comprised a stationers with a printing works at the back of the shop.

The 1930s

Dad gave Mum £2 for the week's housekeeping every Saturday. This was for the six of us, but then four penn'orth of liver provided a meal for us all, along with a mountain of mashed potato, that wonderful vegetable which kept the whole nation going; my generation thrived on it. We had to, at times it was all that kept most families 'filled up'. Some cuts of meat that required stewing for a week and offal were quite cheap enough, and vegetables when they were in season were always to be had on the market stalls in Hildreth Street.

On Saturday nights Mum and I would do the shopping in the open market; in winter by the light of gas flares. At about nine o'clock, because there was little in the way of refrigeration, any unsold meat was auctioned off at Kingstons, the butchers. So if you waited long enough you could get a large family joint for half-a-crown. But who had half-a-crown which was twelve and a half pence in today's money?

My mother made do with £2 a week for many years. Prices seemed to remain pretty steady in those days. Tooting Bec Common was the only open space we had, a green oasis in a sea of roads and houses. Kids pushing pramloads of other kids would make their way to that common whenever the weather was right and I was one of them, pushing the pram with Megan and Barbara in it. Tony, who would never be seen with his sisters, was on the other side of the common with his friends. Sometimes I would meet my cousin Audrey, who had pushed another pramload of kids all the way from Tooting. Prams were very large substantial affairs in those days.

We would be sent up to the common with a bag of broken biscuits and a bottle of lemonade made from sugar, supposedly flavoured with lemon. We were told by Mum to "Stay up there while I have a few moments peace and quiet". Every family seemed to have a dog and without much traffic on the road they roamed at will. We had an airedale-cross bitch called Whiskey, who always seemed to be on heat. No matter how hard Mum tried to keep her in the house she managed, somehow, to get out and would race up to the common to find us. Once there, she would hare madly between Tony on one side of the common and back to me and my pram. She looked a bit like Haley's Comet with a long tail of hopeful dogs streaming behind her. I hated coming home with that pram, with Whiskey and all her suitors in tow.

Mostly, however, we played in the streets with balls, whips and tops, bikes and scooters. Cars, which were mostly owned by professional people like doctors and solicitors, were few and far between. The only real traffic was on the main roads, and a lot of the commercial traffic was horse drawn.

*St Mary's Church, Balham High Road, where many of the family
weddings and christenings took place.*

Our baker had a handcart. To my eternal shame there came an evening in the winter when, after giving me change for what had passed for a sixpence in the dark, he walked to the front door and confronted my mother with the Persian coins which I had been passing off as sixpences for several nights. There was no cake for me for the rest of the week, and I had to go to bed directly after tea. But worst of all, Dad said he did not want to speak to me again for a whole week. We who grew up in the aftermath of the First World War were fortunate in that the majority of us belonged to large families. We had grandparents and many aunts, uncles and cousins. Our parents were born of Victorians whose high moral standards were handed down, along with family loyalty and unity. The characters of our grandmothers especially, were forged on a pretty tough anvil, where childbearing was an endless commitment, and the struggle that followed in the rearing of large families made life tough in the extreme. Our grandmothers were powers to be reckoned with. Life had not defeated them; they had defeated life.

At school we all talked proudly about 'our Grans,' who always remained the vital core of any family. They held their place in the family household and were not shovelled out into the nearest Sunset Home when age and ill health overtook them.

Most of my Dad's family lived quite close in Balham. His mother and father lived in a house in Culverden Road where we all used to gather once a week on Wednesdays. I remember making my way to these gatherings in the afternoon after school. The main living room in Culverden Road was large enough to accommodate a half size dining-billiard table, around which and upon which all the family's activities were centred. On those Wednesday afternoons we sat around it for tea. There was Dad's Mum who we all loved and knew as Nanny, and her six daughters; Winnie, Lily, Dorothy, Ethel, Ivy and Marjorie, who was only seven years older than myself. (Marjorie had a second name, Ceramic, after the name of Dad's troopship. I always thought it very fortunate for her that he had not sailed off to India on *HMS Dreadnought!*) These aunts and my mother would arrive at Culverden Road with the first wave of Nanny's grandchildren.

I always chose to sit at the corner of that billiard table so I could poke my crusts into the loose network of the billiard ball pockets "Now if you don't eat your crusts your hair wont curl" said Nanny. But I was never quite that daft. I knew that nothing would ever change the dead straight unmanageable mouse coloured hair with which I had been blessed. I knew just where to poke those unwanted crusts. On all these Wednesday gatherings Nanny would produce a massive slab of bread pudding which was cut up into squares. Whether it was her expertise in producing it or the quality of the bread that she used, I don't know, but for me there has never been bread pudding like it since those far off Wednesday gatherings at Culverden Road. When the billiard table had its covers taken off, and the pockets had been emptied of crusts and other teatime debris (for by now my cousins had followed my shining example of surplus food disposal) the men of the family, who by this time had arrived home from work, would begin to play billiards. These were the husbands of Dad's eldest sisters and his two brothers Ernie and Eric.

This house and garden backed on to a part of Tooting Bec Common, and I often wonder, should I ever again walk through that part of the Common on a summer night and pass that garden, if I would hear the clink of billiard balls and the sound of Frank Pool, Ivy's first husband, playing the piano amid the sounds of laughter coming through the French windows. During those far off evenings in Culverden Road I experienced, as a child, the feeling of security that belonging to this happy family gave me. My life would be ever cushioned by my grandparents, aunts and uncles.

The highlights of our lives were the wireless, the Balham Picture House, and Woolworths 'The threepenny and sixpenny stores'. All delights were there. We would gaze longingly at the tablets of Lux, Palmolive, and Knights Castille soap, luxuries only for those who could afford not to have to use the large block of Sunlight soap, which we used at the kitchen sink, and shared with the kitchen floor.

When I was about nine years old, I dearly wanted a bicycle for Christmas but all my parents could afford was a pair of roller skates. My disappointment was quite profound, but when I got the hang of the things I spent glorious hours skating down the middle of the roads on the smooth black tar macadam, with only the United Dairies horse to worry about. Now that I am getting quite old, and with all the signs of arthritis setting in, I find that sometimes in my dreams I can still skate with all that joy and freedom down the empty roads of Balham.

The printing business managed to limp on into the 1930s barely providing my mother with the weekly £2 housekeeping money. Printing orders were 'thin on the ground' and chasing up money that was owed for work done often proved fruitless. There were times when bankruptcy almost became a reality and the bailiffs were constant visitors to the Hildreth Street printing works. Amazingly, we children were completely unaware of the desperate financial situation. We only knew there were never any holidays, and clothes were hand-me-downs or remade from garments no longer worn. I remember my grandmother and my Mum making me a coat from a hideous old coat my grandmother had discarded. It was grey with a yellow fleck and very hairy. I hated it, but it had to be worn for at least two winters.

After the First World War, my Dad leased the shop, (right). His army gratuity had gone into stocking it with stationary and books, whilst half became a printers. Lack of trade during the 'depression' of the 1920s forced him to sell up. Stationary and books were a luxury not many could afford. A flattened out envelope was good enough to write a letter on. The printing business just survived, and was moved to the back of Hildreth Street in a windowless building that might once have been a stable. Above the shop is part of Colebrooke Mansions, where my mother and her family lived prior to the First World War.

This is my favourite view of Bedford Hill (below). It is the Bedford Hill I grew up with and is as dear to me and familiar to me as any other place I have known and loved. Parts of it disappeared when they fell victim to the Luftwaffe in the Second World War.

On the right side are the two blinds of Lansdowne's grocery shop. Mr Landsdowne, small, round and stern with his grocer's straw hat and blue and white apron, had four daughters who served in his shop until all hours, even on Sunday mornings. It was always busy in that shop and I dreaded being sent there on an errand as Mr Landsdowne's policy was that no child was ever served whilst an adult was waiting. I seemed to spend hours in that shop standing on one foot and then the other, or tracing patterns with my toe in the sawdust on the floor, endlessly waiting for one of the daughters to be free to serve me. We as children always made way for the 'grown-ups', it was very much their world, and now sadly eighty years later we have come to a complete reversal.

In spite of these hard times, Dad always managed to give me my Saturday penny. One day I took this penny to Woolworths to buy Dad's birthday present, which by his request was a packet of Virginia Stock seeds. I remember him opening the packet to reveal the dust-like seeds and giving me the job of sowing them in the garden with the words "Just make sure that they are all the right way up". Though we children were unaware of the hard times, especially my brother and two sisters who were too young to be aware of the financial situation, I can still hear Dad saying to Mum who was born with an anxiety neurosis, "Put it all out of your mind. Wait until the time comes". I know she found it very difficult to emulate Dad who seemed so easily to just 'switch off' and turn his mind to other things.

When I was in the top class at our local school, where we spent our final years to the age of fourteen, a School journey was being organised for us to visit the Isle of Wight, and stay at Sandown for two weeks. I can remember Dad telling me that it would be impossible for me to go. He was just as unhappy about this as I was. The cost was £2. That was a lot of money to find. But a few days later his brother-in-law gave him a large printing order and on one miraculous lunchtime I remember still, Dad was able to hand across the table to me two £1 notes. I joyfully rushed off to school and, right at the end of the eleventh hour, was included in that 'School journey'. So many times since that sacrifice was made, I would give anything to walk through that front door of No.11 go down the passage into the kitchen, and say to my Dad "Thank you thank you!" and that was only one time.

Days in the Depression

We four children who grew up at 11 Childebert Road were so fortunate; money was scarce but we had two wonderful parents whose humour enlightened the days, especially Dad's. His optimism and faith in the future was boundless. No one could have seen how this ordinary man with his love for caged birds and his simple family life would one day become the well-known and much loved Harry Edwards, a household name known throughout the world.

Life revolved around the simple style of life that we lived at that time, while our parents dealt with the reality of those days, and the endless struggle to make 'both ends meet'. As holidays were more or less out of the question, I would watch my friends going off to exotic sounding places like Weston-Super-Mare in their ankle strap shoes that I would have died for. Long summers drifted by while we four children trailed daily up to Tooting Bec Common and back, but there were days when Mum would make a great pile of egg and tomato sandwiches for lunch and we would all set off for Balham station and later we would reach Epsom Downs. Epsom Downs presented for us a whole new universe where we could run forever, another world from the confines of Tooting Bec Common. We used to leave the Downs after lunch and make for Headley village with its church and tea garden.

There was magic in that tea garden with the scent of all its flowers. Two elderly ladies would fetch us a 'set country tea' on battered old tin trays. The garden had a very intriguing earth closet with twin seats, which was of course still in use, with the squares of neatly cut up newspaper hanging on a string. Headley was in the heart of the country then. I dare not think where it is now. If we wanted anything as children which was beyond the reach of Dad's financial resources, he would tell us that we would have to wait until "the fields were white with daisies." He was as safe as the houses that made up Balham. Well almost.

One day when he took us to Balham Picture House to see the film *Sabu the Elephant Boy*, Megan promptly fell in love with Sabu and desperately wanted an elephant. She whined constantly about having an elephant. She should have known what Dad's reply would be: she could have one "when the fields were white with daisies". On our next trip to Headley, we found that the fields were white

Dad at his press

with daisies, banks of them, ox-eyed daisies everywhere. As soon as Megan saw them she began her endless whine for an elephant, and grizzled about it all day. Eventually, somewhat exasperated, Dad turned to Megan and told her that she would have to wait "until Nelson gets his eye back" It was then, I think, Megan lost all hope.

Most of the local children in Balham including my brother, my two sisters and I went to the same school, Ravenstone. They stayed there from infancy until they were fourteen, by which time they were considered to be fit enough to stand behind shop counters, or work in the United Dairies bottling plant. I thought that working in Woolworths would be like being in heaven. But that was never considered for me. With my number blindness I would have given that much loved local branch severe financial problems. The summers of the 1930s were long and hot, and Tooting Bec Common was the only open space to go. We could not afford to go away on holidays, so the daily trudge to the common went on with the dog and the pram.

During those hot summers front doors were kept open, and striped canvas blinds hung in their place. That could only happen in yesterday's world, while the very threat of Borstal and Reformatory Schools hung heavy in the air, to say nothing of the dreaded 'birch'. Canes hung in bunches from the ceilings of hardware stores. Most homes had one. We lived with the principle of 'Spare the rod and spoil the child'. We had a cane hanging in our scullery; it was seldom used, but I was the one who used to be on the receiving end, and I must say that this fact has never in later years sent me scuttling off to sit in a psychiatrist's chair. I recognised then, as I do now, that I did give my parents a lot of grief. Heaven only knows what I would have got up to, and got away with, in today's incredible society. Somewhere in our social history I feel there must have been a point where the two worlds passed a place where a more realistic compromise could have been made between then and now.

Nothing 'below the belt' was ever discussed. Most of us, throughout our early years, lived in a state of blessed ignorance, and the facts of life passed us by with our childhood. However, strange and contorted half-truths did filter down to us via the school playground. I remember a very embarrassing time, when our dog Whiskey became attached to the policeman's Alsatian from next door, and I announced to my brother and sisters that in nine month's time Whiskey would have puppies. My Mum gave me a clout around the head and said I knew far too much for my own good. So much for sex education. But then in my early teens little had changed since the days when my aunts were getting married in blissful ignorance. My aunt Dorothy before her wedding was busily making her trousseau, which included all in one pyjama suits. It seems her mother and married sisters looked on, without saying a word.

We had Pets

One of the long threads that linked Dad to Balham, and to the rest of his days, was his love of animals and especially birds, and in Balham we had our pets. In the covered market, one could buy any kind of pet or bird. On Saturday mornings it was my job to take the weekly grocery list to Dad at his printing works at the back of Hildreth Street. When he had stopped the printing machines and had locked up we would walk across the road to the market and hand the list over. Later, our groceries would arrive delivered by a boy with a specially large basket attached to his bike to hold the goods. After handing over the list, we would visit Mr Venner, who had a small cubby-hole in the market which was lined with cages of birds. While I helped myself to all the peanuts in the barrel of parrot food, Dad and Mr Venner had long conversations about birds.

Outside the kitchen window, between the wall of our house and a fence, Dad had built an aviary. Through his association with Mr Venner it was full of weavers that cleverly wove knitting wool through the mesh of the chicken wire that was their home, brilliant black and orange bishops, and finches of all kinds and colours.

I used to help Dad rear the young by boiling hen's eggs until the yolks were black for Dad to mix in with something called Eggbisco. I can't remember that he had any luck in rearing young birds. Another arrival at No.11 was a green parrot, called Tommy by his previous owners. It spent most of its time clambering around outside the cage and would transfer to a handy shoulder, if one was standing near. This was a bit like playing Russian roulette as Tommy was a bit of a Jekyll and Hyde. Finding his beak gently nuzzling your cheek was a bit of a heart stopper. One never knew quite what was in that parrot's mind, and his beak was vicious.

Whilst the parrot was still with us, Mr Venner sold Dad a rhesus monkey as a birthday present for Tony. This monkey was called Sally. While I had established an uneasy rapport with the parrot, Sally was my enemy. She loved only Tony and it was wise to keep a distance from the length of her chain as she could and did bite, and heaven help anyone who passed within reach of that chain with a plateful of food. There were one or two occasions when she found herself free of the chain, and the kitchen became a disaster area as she swung from the mantelpiece to furniture, scattering everything in her path, and grabbing anything edible, which she stuffed into the pouches in her cheeks. At these times the parrot would leave the outside of the cage and swarm up the curtains screaming. We did not have television in those days, we had these colourful occasions instead. Mum and Dad coped with them with amazing good humour. When the war came, food for both the monkey and parrot was hard to find and both were returned to Mr Venner, who passed them on to safer hands.

Almost on the catwalk with the 1929 swimwear;
oddly enough it has never made a comeback.

Megan Mum myself and Tony in the garden at no 11.
That garden was a very unrewarding piece of ground but
somehow Mum made it bloom.

Another feathered pet, who demanded a lot of understanding and good humour, was the end result of a yellow fluffy chick bought for tuppence in Balham market. This chick, against all the laws of nature, survived and grew into a cockerel named Andy and lived outside in the garden. He existed in his own frustrated, confined, world without his own kind and became a fighter. He took on anyone who was mad enough to venture out into the garden, or to the outside loo. If you did manage to get to the loo unobserved, you had to 'run the gauntlet' of a major dust-up with a mad cockerel to get back to the kitchen door, and the only way to deal with this was to go to the loo armed with a broom. We had Andy after the outside aviary had been removed and, if anyone tapped on the kitchen window while we were having a meal, Andy would hurl himself at the window in a frenzy. While entertaining us children, it was entertainment with more relish than one of today's horror films, for it was spiced with the uncertainty of just how long the glass in the window would hold out against the weighty onslaught of that frenzied cockerel. The end had to come for Andy. Barbara was terrified of him, the whole family was housebound as far as the garden was concerned. I know that it was with great reluctance that Dad invited his brother-in-law Arthur round to put an end to Andy. Arthur was a country man from Little Bredy in Dorset, who had dealt with country matters all his life. Needless to say, Andy put up a tremendous fight before he was overcome by his experienced executioner. Dad asked Arthur to take Andy away with him. The garden became a very quiet and peaceful place once more, we could go to the loo without the fear of a fight, but a lot of the fire and zest had gone out of our lives.

Tony and Sally

We had a succession of dogs and cats, until we arrived at Burrows Lea. Many years were to pass before that came about, but when it did, Dad's interest in birds and animals continued. Dad was forever hanging food up outside for the wild birds, while the Burrows Lea parrot called Poppet was calling for Heatherbell, the Persian cat from within. There were also outside aviaries for a number of budgerigars. But who in those Balham days could have foreseen a place like Burrows Lea?

However, while we still lived in Balham, there was an odd moment that I can recall. In my late teens I pretended that I could read tea leaves. At this time teabags had not come into use in this country so tea leaves were scattered around our cups in all sorts of images and patterns. If you were fussy about this, you used a tea strainer when pouring from the pot. I read Mum's cup one afternoon and told her that she would live once again in the country, and have not one house cow, but two. My mother, whose only view outside the kitchen and scullery window was on to a yellow brick wall of the house next door, hankered after her days spent in Dorset during the First World War, when she and her father ran a herd of Jersey cows for the Gribble estate at Kingston Russell, Longbredy.

Oddly enough, this tea-leaf reading came true. At Burrows Lea, Mum had two 'house cows,' Honey Dew and Cleopatra, and Cleopatra was a Jersey. I don't think I was a budding clairvoyant

Dad 'composing' i.e, hand setting type

at the time I was reading tea leaves, just someone with a creative imagination, but who knows? Such a vision in a terraced house in Balham was too far-fetched to be considered as anything near likely, but it happened. A long time ahead, but it happened.

By the time our days at Burrows Lea came to their end, there had been a long history of dogs, cats, birds, cows and horses under the care of Burrows Lea. A paddock had been set aside for horses needing a temporary home. Towards the end of his time at Burrows Lea, Dad acquired a load of monkeys which were on loan to him.

Dad in his billet in Kermanshah during the First World War

Forthcoming events cast their shadows before them

The words 'spiritual healer' were generally unknown and unthought of in those early Balham years. Dad was a printer by day and a politician at night, for it was then that he would go to his meetings wearing his black overcoat, white silk scarf, and bowler hat.

When I look back on his life, I can see a definite plan set out for him to follow, like a blue print, each stage set and ready to lead into the next. They were to bring him to the point when he would demonstrate to the world the power of spiritual healing. When Paul Miller called his book on Dad's life *Born to Heal*, he summed it all up in just those few words. However my father was not only born to heal, he was to put healing on the map, to present to the world through his public demonstrations that a healing force truly existed and was there for whoever wanted to use it. To achieve all this, he was to walk on to the largest platforms and confront the largest audiences in this country and abroad. His training ground was to be on the political platforms of London, for he had the ambition to enter Parliament.

"Forthcoming events" someone once wrote, "cast their shadows before them." So it was during the First World War. During Dad's travels in Persia, he was surprised to find local people approached him with a form of expectation that he could cure their ills. He had no medical knowledge worth speaking of and his medical supplies were meagre, yet they brought their sick and chronically ill to him on stretchers and laid them outside his tent. Naturally, he did what he could for them and was further surprised when recoveries took place. News of these travelled ahead of him and, in the course of time, he learned that people everywhere were calling him 'Hakim' which means 'Healer'. When finally Dad had to return to England they followed him crying, "You are our father and our mother! Do not leave us." This was something he failed to understand.

On Sundays, when we were sitting around the kitchen table at No.11, Dad would recount his experiences in Persia and his encounters with tribesmen and their families from the Persian hills and countryside. Of course with hindsight we can see that they had a healer in their midst, but the healer did not know this himself.

On one of these occasions around the Sunday lunch table, Dad told us that he had been a neighbour to a wealthy merchant in Baghdad, who like other wealthy merchants in the area had a harem. One evening he heard a lot of screaming coming from the harem courtyard and saw several women struggling there with one who was trying to throw herself into a well. Running across the flat roof that separated him from the women, and dropping down into the courtyard, he soon discovered that the woman had been bitten by a scorpion. He put his hand over the bite and the screaming stopped. At this point Dad would look around at us all and say "And do you know, I could actually feel the heat and pain being drawn from her." He went on to tell us that the next day the merchant, his neighbour, rode into the camp with a retinue of henchmen armed to the teeth. Everyone expected trouble. One does not invade a harem lightly. But there was no cause for concern: to my father's relief he was thanked very substantially for his intervention.

Not one of us said "Well you must have the power of healing". Such words were unknown to us. It was to be a long time before George Daisley and Bertha Harris, both famous clairvoyants in their day, were to say similar words to him. There was much work and preparation before that time was to come, but the plan was unfolding as we lived our lives that revolved around the printer and prospective politician, who was our Dad.

In pursuit of his political aims he was a frequent visitor on Sundays to Speakers' Corner at Hyde Park. He often took me with him, travelling there on the top of a London bus. There was so much he would point out to me. I remember in particular a golden girl poised on one foot on a high domed roof in the city. She had her arms outstretched in a classic ballet position. Dad used to tell me that when I was not looking she changed legs. I believed him. We would go past the Kings garden and on to Hyde Park where sheep were kept in railed enclosures. When Dad mounted the Liberal stand, the crowd would gather for him as they did for no one else. I would find myself being pushed further and further back until he was far away on his stand. He drew the crowds but they were not easy to handle.

As the crowds of people surrounded the political stands in Hyde Park, the heckling became loud and bitter. The First World War was not far behind us, and this land 'fit for heroes' to live in had fallen sadly short of all expectations. It was not an unusual sight to see a legless ex-serviceman propped up outside against the wall of the Bedford pub in Bedford Hill in Balham selling matches, or a blind man wearing his service medal ribbons playing a mouth organ for pennies. In those days election fever ran high. All public meetings were attended with much enthusiasm. We only had newspapers and the wireless (if you were lucky enough to own one) for any political guidance. The members of our large family would sit around the kitchen table addressing envelopes and enclosing Dad's election address with those familiar headings POVERTY, UNEMPLOYMENT, and HOUSING. Nearly all the houses in London had an election poster displayed of one colour or another.

Dad kept a book of press cuttings taken from the years he spent fighting the Liberal cause. I found one with the heading A MONSTER GATHERING. It reads as follows:

"By far the largest gathering in recent years in Camberwell was held on Tuesday, February 28th, at the Old Kent Road Baths when new voters were invited to meet Mr and Mrs Edwards. Every seat was full, and every available space and foot of standing room was occupied. In addition at least another 1,000 people were unable to gain admittance."

The press called Dad "The Grand Young Man of Camberwell". Camberwell (North) being the constituency for which he was elected by his party to stand for Parliament. During the election campaigns of 1929 and 1935 Dad's election posters rolled off his Wharfdale press at the printing works, and I have some of them to this day. One of the greatest spin-offs of having him involved in politics was the amount of mail that came through our letter box addressed to H.J. Edwards Esquire. This was the usual form of address, and letters would end with "I am your obedient servant" so and so. I would welcome these large bulky envelopes as I knew that Dad would hand over to me the pages with a blank side, and this meant paper to draw on. It is hard to believe that though he was a printer, paper at home was scarce. The paper waste at the printers was only in thin slivers. I roamed the house looking for paper to draw on and I removed all the fly leaves and title pages from every book I could find, so that when you opened the cover you were confronted with Chapter One. I still grieve today when I see good paper going to waste. There seemed to be so little of it in those Balham days, when I craved for something to draw on.

When Mum and Dad went off to their political meetings in the evenings, they left me in charge of my brother and two sisters while I was still a schoolgirl. This would be frowned upon today, but then we were out working at the age of fourteen, so we grew up quickly. Families were large, and it was not unusual for the older children to have the responsibility for the younger ones. When

*The crowd beginning to gather for Dad
at Speakers' Corner*

The crowd does not seem to be gathering for me

Mum and Dad left, Megan and Barbara were already in bed and I was given the usual instructions from Dad. I was not to play with the fire. I was to see that Tony went to bed at 8 o'clock, I was to go to bed at 8.30, and to see that all the electric lights were turned off. My Mum would say "And don't let that dog get on the bed!" I did not play with the fire, but I made my brother go to bed by 7.30 by threatening to smash the electric light bulb and blow the house up. Electricity had just been installed in our home, a new mysterious wonder. Seeing my brother scampering up the stairs in fear half-an-hour before he needed to, was oddly very satisfying. I did not go to bed at 8.30. I would wait by the wireless for Geraldo and his dance music to come on at 9 o'clock. I would go to bed at 9.30 (with the dog) switching all the lights out as I went.

The politician facing changes

WITH grateful thanks for the splendid help you rendered to our Cause during the past General Election.

Although we did not succeed in winning the fight we have added considerably to our strength in numbers and friends, and so fortified we shall go on with renewed courage and vigour for the victory to come.

So long as wrongs remain to be righted, and grievances to ad-
just so must Liberalism live.

To serve this Cause is to serve humanity and to this end may we continue.

With renewed thanks,
We are
Yours sincerely,

Harry Godwin

Electricity cost money and lights left on unnecessarily wasted money. This little bit of Balham life has followed me for all my days and my Dad was the same throughout the later years of his life. Even when money was no longer a problem he would be very upset if someone left the hall light or the light on the stairs on. Of course when Mum and Dad returned home from their meeting the first thing they would hear as they came through the front door would be the dog jumping off the bed.

Eventually "The Grand Young Man of Camberwell" came through the fires of political campaigning with all the enthusiasm of his beliefs and intentions which would bring a better life for the people he was representing; but the Liberal star was setting. The election results for North Camberwell, though well up, were not sufficient to win the seat.

Mr. H. J. EDWARDS speaking in Hyde Park.   *" Daily News " Photo.*

H. J. EDWARDS

the Prospective

LIBERAL   CANDIDATE

will speak at

ARTHUR STREET L.C.C. SCHOOLS,

Old Kent Road near Canal Bridge

on THURSDAY, APRIL 4th, at 8-30 p.m.

on

"WE CAN CONQUER
UNEMPLOYMENT"

Please note the public meeting will not commence until
8-30 p.m., when an important announcement will be
made.   Questions Invited.

NEW VOTERS SPECIALLY INVITED

P.T.O.

Election poster

An election display in North Camberwell

George Daisley, the famous clairvoyant, who clearly predicted Dad's future.

Is there anybody there?

By the early 1930s Dad had demonstrated his ability to command the attention of large audiences at political meetings but his political aspirations were to give way to another, more dominant interest, Spiritualism, which would change the course his life dramatically.

Now was the time to tell the healer he was a healer.

At this time Spiritualism was popular and Spiritualist churches were scattered liberally throughout London. The owners of large houses opened their rooms for church services and so-called development circles, which gave participants the opportunity to explore and, hopefully, develop their ability to communicate with those in the next world.

Spirit Guides became popular and as well-known as their mediums and the *Psychic News* enjoyed a thriving readership. It even had its own news placards quoting the sage pronouncements of the famous Silver Birch (the Red Indian guide of Maurice Barbanell, the editor of *Psychic News*) along with Red Cloud, the guide of Estelle Roberts, who was the country's leading clairvoyant at the time. I once heard Maurice Barbanell on the radio explaining to a slightly bemused interviewer why it was that Red Indians featured so strongly as Spirit Guides. It was, he explained their strong attunement with the Earth's forces, their great sensitivity to a plane beyond the one they were inhabiting, and their rapport with nature. They lived in a world within worlds. I believe that the Aborigines have a similar elusive understanding, but so far I have never heard of anyone with an Aborigine Spirit Guide.

The day came when 'Tommy' Layton, a close friend of the family came to No11 with the news that she had spent an amazing evening at a Spiritualist Meeting held in a house in the road next to ours, Cloudsdale Road. She described an evening of clairvoyance, but Dad, the politician, was very sceptical about it all. Spiritualism and Spiritualists were the butt of music hall jokes, second only in popularity to those about mothers-in-law. "Come with me and see for yourselves" said Tommy. So Mum and Dad went with her to the next meeting. They went again and again. Dad tried to disprove all that he was hearing, to try and work out the tricks that must be played to produce so much evidence that there were indeed two worlds.

Then came the time when I started to accompany him to a small Spiritualist church on Sunday mornings. It was run by a Mr and Mrs Jarman. I remember how very embarrassed I was when one morning Dad took his place on the platform and gave an invocation. It was the first time I had heard him mention God. My parents had never been churchgoers, and religion, like the facts of life, was never mentioned in our house; politics yes, God never. However all that was going to change; my parents had become Spiritualists, and to my great shame our home became the Balham Psychic Research Society. What would they say at school, if they knew?

Very little was discussed in the way of religion in my home. Only my grandfather, Dad's father spoke to me about his thoughts on life and death. He did not believe in a 'here-after'. I remember him saying "As long as you, my grandchildren live and have your children, that is how I will live on. That is a law of the universe. One day you will discover that these laws outweigh anything you will learn from the church". It was heavy stuff for a schoolgirl at that time, but I have come to understand the sense of those words.

It was Bertha Harris who, at one of the meetings in Cloudsdale Road, said to Dad, "Did you not know that you are born to heal?" He received similar messages from others. It was, for example, the well-known George Daisley at the Hartfield Spiritualist Church in Wimbledon, who told Dad that he was destined to become a great healer, and as a result of his work life would go through great changes for him, and his family.

"You have the Power to Heal"

In the development circles that were held in our home and elsewhere, the same message to the effect that Dad was a healer kept coming through. Then came the crucial point when he concentrated his thoughts for the first time on a patient, whom he heard was in Brompton Hospital suffering from advanced tuberculosis. During a period of meditation he focused his thoughts on this patient and found himself walking down a hospital ward, with his attention focused on a certain bed.

Dad would tell us all about this experience. He found it profoundly moving and firmly believed that this was his first encounter with so-called 'astral travelling'. Though many times he was to go on similar journeys, that particular one was to remain with him always. Within twenty four hours of his astral visit to the hospital, the patient had begun to show significant signs of improvement: the haemorrhaging of the lungs had diminished, and the blood and sputum showed no signs of the causative bacterium.

Other cures of a similar kind were to follow, erasing from my fathers mind whatever early doubts he may have been harbouring about his healing. Although life went on much the same as usual in our Balham home, stories of Dad's patients recovering against all odds were becoming increasingly a part of the background to our daily activities. I remember Hetty and Gladys Cudd, who lived in Sistova Road, Balham. Dad came to know about them in a very odd way. Hetty had been to a medium on the other side of London as her sister Gladys, who was a young girl, had a terminal illness. The medium, who was also a healer, told Hetty to get in touch with one Harry Edwards who lived close to her. With the help of a telephone directory she found him. This was not difficult as telephones were quite rare in ordinary houses, and the whole of London's telephone subscribers could be found in one book. As far as Dad was concerned he was hardly known so far afield as a healer and was somewhat taken aback when Hetty walked into his shop and told her story.

Sistova Road was only about five minutes walk away from No.11. When Dad went to visit her he found that straw had been laid in the road outside her house to deaden the sound of the mostly horse-drawn traffic. He was shown upstairs to where Gladys was lying and put his hands on each side of her head. As he did so he felt the healing force flow through him, producing a sense of exhilaration such as he had never experienced before. Gladys recovered. Hetty also sought Dad's help with a problem of her own, a malformed bone in her foot. I remember, when I was walking with her down Bedford Hill many months later, she told me that, after receiving healing from Dad she was able, for the first time in her life, to buy a pair of shoes from a shop instead of having them specially made for her. "Your father did that for me," she said, "You have a wonderful father."

In our own road lived the Ramsey family. Betty Ramsey was my friend and I often saw her setting off with her mother to the Streatham Astoria, a new up-to-date cinema, which from Betty's description made the Balham picture house sound like a mud hut. For me the Streatham Astoria had become a shrine I longed to visit. Betty's brother was in a wheelchair suffering from some sort of paralysis. Everyday Dad would visit the Ramsey home and Mrs Ramsey said to me one day. "When your Dad comes into the house, it is just like the sunshine breaking through. His visits make such a difference to my son. Your Dad lightens up his life." Wonderful words, which I remember still, but at that time I would much rather have had an invitation to the Streatham Astoria.

Letters began to arrive at No.11 asking Dad for his help. Little did we know that these were the forerunners of the fourteen million or so that were yet to be written and sent to our Dad. We children gradually began to realise that he was no longer just the local printer and stationer and our Dad; he was becoming the man everyone was looking for. The man who could heal.

At a large meeting in London a document was passed round the platform for everyone's signature. Dad and his neighbour, a man of his own age, both produced fountain pens. Both pens were of the same make and colour and both had their owner's signatures engraved upon them. They bore the same inscription: H J Edwards. But this was not all; both men it turned out were called Harry James.

Thus began a friendship that was to last many years 'HJ' as we came to know Dad's namesake, was sponsoring the mediumship of a young man whose name was George Daisley and whose power of clairvoyance was second to none. There were two mediums who dominated the headlines in the *Psychic News* during those heady days of the 1930s when very large audiences followed them into the larger halls and Spiritualist churches. They were George Daisley and Estelle Roberts. I did not get to see or hear Estelle Roberts, but I did come to know George and HJ well. They both became such good friends of my parents, and it was George who gave Dad so many positive messages about his future as a healer. He also told Dad that he would write a book.

Remembering Dad's typewriter in his office, this must have been a very daunting prophesy. With the large white keys set into brass rings, it was rather like trying to type with a birdcage with long steel arms delivering the keys with a loud clunk. I had spent many happy hours hammering away on that typewriter, which probably had not improved its performance. However write a book Dad did, and it was to be the first of many.

The drawing of Black Cloud, Jack Webber's Guide who has been described as a North American Indian of the Mohawk Tribe and who took direct control of the séances and the medium's body.

One evening shortly before Jack's death, Dad and Jack were talking in the kitchen of No. 11 when Dad picked up a piece of paper and started to draw, without stopping for any correction or for any creative thought of his own while this drawing of Black Cloud took place.

The surprising thing here, which was noted at the time, is the likeness of Black Cloud to Jack Webber himself. It seemed as if the two faces merge here. The arrival of this drawing surprised Dad as it did the rest of us, as it portrays a skill outside Dad's artistic province. It seemed to set a seal on the very close association between Black Cloud and Dad, which Dad greatly valued.

John (Jack) Boaden Webber

Along with all the fine mediums of the day, my father as a speaker as well as a healer was becoming well-known. The *Psychic News* carried many a report of his success as a healer, and the editor Maurice Barbanell was coming to be another visitor to No 11.

One day my parents went to Wales. They had heard of the mediumship of Jack Boaden Webber. They made that journey more than once, and attended séances given by Jack in London. A strong friendship developed between him and my father that was to bring about one of the most extraordinary phases of our lives.

Jack had been a coal miner. A victim of the very poor education received in his mining village during the First World War, he found himself down the mines at the age of fourteen scarcely able to read or write. When he was courting his girlfriend Rhoda Evans he attended the development circles held by her parents. He quickly went into a trance and his extraordinary mediumship began to develop. By the time he and Rhoda were married and had two young sons, he was holding séances that were being talked and written about within the Spiritualist movement.

It was at this time that Mum and Dad were making their Welsh visits. Jack confided in Dad that he wanted to leave Wales and work in London and asked if Dad could find him a suitable house. I don't know what plan or purpose was afoot to bring Jack into our lives, but in the extraordinary way these things happen, No.13 Childebert Road, became vacant. It was not long before Mr and Mrs Evans, Jack, Rhoda and family moved in next door. Jack's séance room was established in one of the ground floor rooms. Beside Jack's stout Windsor chair with arms, there would be a coil of ropes, two large steel cones with a broad band of luminous paint round the wider end and two plaques of four-ply wood, also covered in luminous paint, and a tambourine. Apart from these things, only chairs for about twenty people lined the walls.

Jack, small, slight, and sandy haired would enter this room when everyone was seated. Then would come the request for someone to tie him up. Sometimes two people would do this. Bernard Grey of the *Sunday Pictorial* wrote, "I bound him to his chair hand and foot, with knots and double knots a sailor had taught me, and just to make sure that he could not wriggle out and back again without my knowing it, I tied lengths of household cotton from the ropes to the chair legs. And I sewed up the front of his jacket with stout thread". Colin Evans, another journalist, wrote "I scrutinised very closely the tying of the medium's hands, arms and ankles to the chair by rope. Even had it been possible to slip his arm from the rope, and later to put it back, it would have been an utter and complete impossibility to arrange precisely the same angle of the crossing of the rope there, except by using both hands to do so, and to be able to see clearly while doing it, and therefore an utter impossibility for the medium himself to achieve, in the light or in darkness, or for any other person to accomplish in the dark."

Before he was tied in the chair, his coat was stitched all down the front so that it was an absolutely tight fit and could not possibly be taken off or put on again. After the séance it took some minutes to cut it away with scissors.

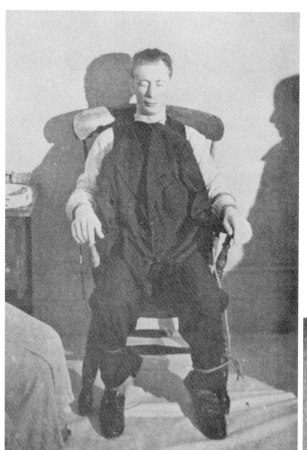

*The removal of Jack's coat,
one of the major features of his séances.*

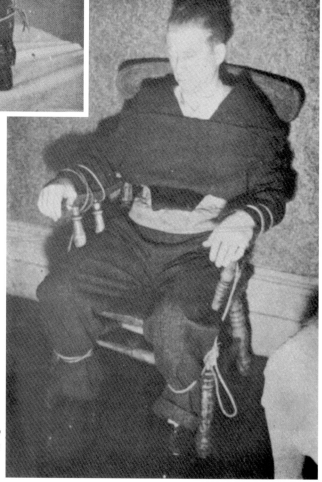

*It is quite impossible to reproduce this effect.
When the photograph was developed
I remember Dad and others spending ages trying to
see how this could be done. In fact it could only be
done by dematerialising the body and bringing
the coat through and up.*

30

Jack's guide was a Red Indian called Black Cloud and he was in total control of the events that followed. Once the ropes were tied, Jack went into a total trance, hands were linked around the room and the lights turned out. Within seconds, two trumpets as they were called, would rise slowly and would then move around the room with astonishing speed. They would come to rest at ceiling level in opposite corners of the room before moving swiftly again, so swiftly that the luminous paint appeared in long bands and they would weave bright patterns in the darkness of the room, skimming past each other but never touching. Then, quite suddenly, they would come to rest touching someone lightly or hovering before a face. These trumpets were used for 'direct voice' messages, which means that as the trumpet hovered before you, a voice you knew and loved would speak to you through it.

Over the months messages were given in different languages to foreign sitters, one even in faultless Latin readily recognized by the sitters. Jack Webber, through little fault of his own, though he did admit that he spent more time in the hills than he did at school, was an illiterate man who depended on Dad for all his written work. His knowledge of the King's English was very limited, as was his vocabulary. Yet through these trumpets would come faultless messages given in foreign languages from all over the world.

Colin Evans wrote, "Repeatedly the medium's control (Black Cloud) called for 'light' and every time the light was switched on instantly, and as it was switched on the trumpets would sink with a fairly rapid movement, but not so rapidly as a falling body unsupported towards the floor, and when the light was on the trumpets were usually just reaching the floor, but still in movement, and continued moving for a moment or two, once for almost half a minute, with gentle movements, obviously intelligently controlled". Later in the sitting, Black Cloud would ask for the light to be put on and every one would see the medium still tightly bound in his coat. The light would go off and within seconds the coat would be heard falling to the floor. On would go the lights and there would be Jack, sitting roped in his shirt sleeves, still in a heavy trance. There are many photographs taken in infrared light showing the coat, partly dematerialised being removed. I can remember still the wonder and excitement of those photographs when they were developed.

The two luminous plaques, which were often used to show the medium still in his chair by outlining his form, would then float about the room showing the sitters faces and linked hands. Levitation also took place during these sittings when Jack, tied in his chair, would be removed with the chair and dumped into the middle of the circle. During these levitations Black Cloud would speak and his voice would be heard from high above the sitters.

On Thursday evenings, in our own Sanctuary at No.11. Jack continued his development under the directions of Black Cloud. These sittings were held in red light and photographs were taken showing the build up of ectoplasm, which formed the 'voice box' for the direct messages. They showed the coat in various stages of dematerialisation and I can remember still the wonder and excitement of those photographs, probably the only ones of their type in the world. They were published in a book, 'The Mediumship of Jack Webber', written by my father, as foretold by George Daisley.

Jack took great risks when he went into a trance. Though everyone was told to link hands and not to touch anything, there was always the one person who did. One of Dad's associates, who should have known better as he was well versed in the procedures of a séance room, picked up a trumpet that had come to rest on his knee. Immediately Black Cloud asked for the lights and there was Jack sitting there in his ropes with blood pouring from his nose. The force of the power which controlled the trumpet was returned to his body with such a violent impact when the trumpet had been picked up, it caused a lengthy haemorrhage. Many well-known faces visited both our houses. Some came to deride and scoff hoping to catch Jack untying ropes and wandering about swinging trumpets around, but the phenomena they witnessed astounded them. *"Cassandra"* of the Daily Mirror wrote "I came to scoff, but the smile is on the other side of my face".

Quotes from Cassandra's article on a Jack Webber séance printed in the Daily Mirror on February 28th 1939.

CASSANDRA GOT A SURPRISE AT A SÉANCE.

I claim I can bring as much scepticism to bear on Spiritualism as any newspaper writer living, and that's a powerful load of scepticism these days. I haven't got an open mind on the subject-I'm a violent, prejudiced unbeliever with a limitless ability to leer at the unknown. At least, I was till last Saturday. And then I got a swift, sharp, ugly jolt that shook most of my pet sneers right out of their sockets.

Picture to yourself a small room in a typical suburban house. In one corner a radio-gramaphone. In the centre a ring of chairs. And at the far end an armchair. About a dozen people filed in and sat in the circle, I hope they wont mind my saying it, but they struck me as a credulous collection that would have brought tears of joy to a share pusher's eyes. Almost everyone a genuine customer for a lovely phony gold brick.

They sat down and the medium, a young Welsh ex-miner, was the roped to the armchair. The photographer and I stood outside the circle. The lights went out and we sailed rapidly into the unknown, and we opened up with a strangled prayer. The circle of believers answered with "All hail the Power of Jesu's Name" and I was told we were "on the brink" I thought we were in Cockfosters, Herts, but I soon began to doubt it when trumpets sprayed with luminous paint shot around the room like fishes in a tank. They hovered like pike in a stream and then swam slowly about. Somebody put a record on and we were soon bellowing "Daisy, Daisy, give me your answer do" The trumpets beat time and hurled themselves against the ceiling.

A bell rang.

There was considerable excited laughter. A tambourine with "God is Love" written on it became highly unreasonable and flew up noisily round our heads. The rough breathing from the medium continued and a faint tapping sound heralded a voice speaking from one of the trumpets that was well adrift from its moorings. A faint childish voice said that it was "very very happy". More voices spoke. Water was splashed about (there was none in the room when we started) and books took off from their shelves.

Table moved.

The medium remained lashed to his chair. A clockwork train ran across the floor. Suddenly a heavy table slowly left the ground. The man who was sitting next to it said calmly "The table's gone" The photographer released his flash. At no time did the medium move from his chair. I swear it. The table landed with a thump in the middle of the circle. A book that was on it remained in position.I pledge my word that not a soul in the room touched it. It was so heavy that it needed quite a husky fellow to lift it. I felt the weight of it afterward.

What price cynicism? What price heresy?

Don't ask me what it all means, but you cant tell me now that these strange and rather terrifying don't happen. I was there. I saw them. I went to scoff. But the laugh is sliding slowly round to the other side of my face.

This article was accompanied with the photograph taken of the table being levitated with the medium securely roped in his chair.

All these objects were apported at Jack Webber séances. Above brass bird, stone Buddha, mosaic ornament and Egyptian ornament of Osiris, a deep blue stone.

In the early days of our association with Jack Webber, I was still at school and not allowed to take part in any of the sittings or the development circle. I was sent to bed early on those Thursday nights when it was being held in our house, with the *Schoolgirl* a magazine for tuppence, but for me such a rare treat. Later I was allowed to stay up and make the tea for the members of the development circles. I was rather frivolous in the early days. One night I decided to put Black Cloud to the test. While waiting for the circle to end I climbed on to the dresser and tapped the wall adjoining the Sanctuary very loudly with a pair of scissors. Black Cloud would either have to acknowledge these taps as part of the séance or 'grass' on me. I waited in some trepidation for the last hymn to be sung, and everyone was out drinking tea. I knew that Dad would be far from pleased if he knew that I was manufacturing psychic phenomena. The knocks were not mentioned. Black Cloud had made no comment and they were passed over. I must have been pretty sure of my ground trifling with a very high-powered Red Indian spirit.

On one of these occasions, though I did not see it happening, a small brass stork that came from Persia was dematerialised from the mantelpiece of the room where I was sitting and apported through the wall into the next room where the sitting was being held. Other objects were apported into that circle, the most precious of which was an Egyptian amulet that the British Museum claimed, when Dad took it there, to be 3,500 years old. My father treasured this for the rest of his life.

As the months went by and I grew a little older and started work, I was allowed to sit in the development circles. It is strange to think that now I must be the only person left who has first hand knowledge of Jack Webber and his mediumship. I can recall the very smell of ectoplasm, a dank earthy smell, but most of all I remember the voice of Reuben, another of Jack's guides. One of the trumpets would hover in the middle of the circle and the powerful voice of Reuben would come through. It had a tremendous power of its own and had all the quality of Paul Robeson. As Dad subsequently wrote in his book the Mediumship of Jack Webber. "At all times the voice was of full loud speaker strength possessing a quality of tone that is distinctive, and which the medium is incapable of reproducing. Reuben has sung continuously for an hour without cessation with such vigour that any throat would have become exhausted and hoarse".

During the time he lived at No. 13, Jack had a hobby. Every day he would go to the covered market in Bedford Hill and work the cranes in what passed as the amusement arcade. His skill in operating these cranes which were supposed to scoop up all sorts of treasures from a mass of coloured stones was uncanny. He used to bring home a collection of cigarette cases, compacts, lighters, bracelets and dubious watches that never worked for more than five minutes, all highly coloured trash. He gave me a compact. It was an oblong, flat two-sided affair, and bright scarlet. One half opened, and under a cotton mesh I kept a supply of Coty Apricot face powder. The opposite side opened revealing a cigarette case, I was not allowed to smoke, but filled it with cigarettes just the same. They became well impregnated with the scent of the face powder. From a bright red tassel at the end of the compact one could pull out a heavily scented, gritty, raspberry coloured lipstick, and that did not do much for the cigarettes either. I remember offering one of these cigarettes to a very promising young chap, who partnered me at the Nina Mason School of Dancing, in Balham High Road. I seem to have lost sight of him after that. Those were the nights when we learned to dance to the strict tempo of Victor Silvestor's ballroom dance music.

Detail of the ornament dedicated to Osiris that was 'apported' into one of Jack Webber's séances

In 1940, the day came that George Daisley had forecast; Jack would leave our lives as quickly as he had come into them. Jack died suddenly with spinal meningitis. Dad had tried, and hoped that his powers of healing would prevail, and that Jack would recover. But this did not happen. Ironically enough, another case of meningitis was brought to Dad's attention at about the same time. A perfect stranger received healing and astounded the medical staff in his Portsmouth hospital by making a recovery that threw all their textbooks to the winds.

The evening before Jack's funeral, I came home from work and found, on arriving at the Balham Underground station, a great crowd of Welsh people milling around the ticket collector, asking if he knew how they could find the home of their relation, Jack Webber. They all believed that he had made a fortune in London, and had come all the way from Wales to be present at the "share out". I fled home, and my mother and I watched this tribe from Jack's valley pour into Childebert Road, and into the house next door. The next day was Jack Webber's funeral. Jack should have been a very wealthy man, he earned around £20 at every sitting. So it was a surprise to learn that his family was left destitute. We could only conclude that it had all vanished into the crane machines in Balham market.

During the time Jack was with us, we did not think too much about why he had been sent into our lives. His amazing mediumship would have been recognized and developed anywhere with the help of so many people, who were around at that time and anxious to help him. But it was my father to whom he turned, and it was the house next door that became vacant, when he wanted to move. In retrospect, it would all seem to be a part of my father's own spiritualistic development. Perhaps the liaison and friendship between the two men and Black Cloud was necessary as a part of the training my father needed for his future work. It may well have been there was a need to convince him further that the power he was to believe in so absolutely for the rest of his life must be demonstrated in this way, to prove to him beyond doubt that there are forces beyond man's understanding, knowledge or control, waiting to be used. That he could heal was now something that Dad accepted, but the task that lay before him was tremendous. He was only beginning to understand a little of the power that lay behind his Healing. The evidence that Jack brought in such abundance surely was to be the cornerstone of Dad's belief in his own powers.

Comparatively little time had passed since his first sceptical visit to the house in Cloudsdale Road, and since his first healings took place. He had now heard faultless English spoken through the trumpet, fluent French, German, Dutch and even Latin, spoken through the mediumship of an illiterate Welsh miner, who had difficulty in writing his own name. He had seen perfect faces formed out of ectoplasm, materialising out of nothing and dissolving away into nothing. To have heard that powerful voice of Reuben pouring from one of the trumpets and feeling the very furniture vibrate with the tremendous power of that voice was something none of us would ever forget. That voice would have guaranteed Jack a fortune in the recording studios or in the world's theatres. To know that an object had been dematerialised in one room and passed through the wall into the next, and to be able to record on film the dematerialising process taking place, and of objects in levitation; those were some of the things we marvelled at. We were given an insight into the powers that at this time are so far beyond our understanding. There is no doubt that as time passes and man evolves, they will be ours to use.

In much later years when Dad was watching 'Star Trek' he turned to me at those well known words 'Beam me up Scottie' and said "You see, given time all things are possible".

Glass slides were made from the many photographs taken at Jack Webber's sittings and Dad gave many talks on this subject. Thirty-seven years later, after the days of Jack Webber, when Dad and I sat alone together in the sitting room at Burrows Lea, we went once more through those slides for the last time, and the two of us lived again those many incredible months, when Jack lived next door and every day seemed to be a day of great expectation borne along on a tide of energy.

Decca the recording company did make a recording of Reuben singing and several copies were produced, but time and the nature of those old 78 records ensured their gradual disappearance. 'Lead Kindly Light' was on one side of the record and 'Lead Thou Me On' was on the other. 'Danny Boy' Jack's favourite as well as mine, was not recorded by Decca, and now only exists in my memory. A few years before Dad left us, one of these precious recordings came into his possession via someone in the Evans family. Dad was elated. He got someone to pack it up very carefully and send it to a recording studio. Whoever that someone was, they were not careful enough and that last remaining recording arrived at the studio in pieces. I suppose recording technology in 1940 was somewhat limited by today's standards and a lot of Reuben was lost in that early recording. Today would be a different story, but then Jack would not have survived in today's world. He would have been hounded by the press and the media, who would surely have destroyed him.

In recent times there seem to have been some moves to disassociate Spiritual Healing from Physical Mediumship, almost as if Spiritual Healing would be downgraded in some way. I doubt whether we will ever see another medium like Jack Webber, so I think it has been worthwhile recording this story, for he was a very important part of the unfolding blueprint, part of a major plan, and I can hear my Dad saying, "It was meant to be".

Seventy years have passed since those remarkable days when Jack was with us and I can still hear the voice of Reuben and the words of Black Cloud as though they were people I once knew and loved and cannot forget. They bring back the memories of the journeys Dad and I took through the blackout and the rubble of our war damaged city to the awaiting audiences in various halls and Spiritualist churches to show those incredible slides that told so vividly the story of Jack Webber and his Mediumship.

Jack Webber died in 1940. The Second World War had just begun, but while he was with us, and during the years prior to his arrival, the world was moving towards another great catastrophe and the signs had been many. Fascism was rearing its very ugly face, though in some circles it was seen as quite a respectable philosophy.

Adolf Hitler who had done so much for the economy of Germany was seen as quite an agreeable gentleman. The Duke and Duchess of Windsor, as well as many heads of State, brought home glowing accounts of Hitler's new Germany, but the insidious overtones were always there. As in Germany, Jew baiting here in this country was becoming a popular Fascist pastime. We saw Mussolini's army march into Abbysinia and the proud figure of Emperor Heille Sellassie, exiled from his land, on our newsreels in the local cinemas, when he visited London. The expression 'jackboot' was now appearing in our vocabulary. Fascism was becoming a real and almost tangible presence in our world. The Spanish Civil War broke out in 1936 and newsreels showing us the bombing of Spanish cities gave us a foretaste of what was to come, but the ferocity of the attacks shown on those newsreels was but a pale shadow of what was to befall Warsaw, London, Coventry, and eventually Berlin and Dresden.

It was another case of 'Forthcoming events casting their shadows before them' and the world stood in the path of a great eclipse. In the lengthening shadows of 1939, when the Spanish Republic had been crushed, German troops entered Vienna, the Sudetenland and finally Prague This had the effect of shredding the Munich agreement (Peace in our time) so painfully agreed the previous September. War was only a matter of months away. On the 1st of September the Nazis invaded Poland.

The start of the war

History came and went during my first fifteen years in a very benign fashion. Mrs Wallace Simpson arrived, a King abdicated, so we had a new king and a coronation I was just over fifteen when the Munich agreement was signed in 1938, promising us "Peace in our time". History was about to pass us quietly-by once more, but instead, history for my generation was about to erupt, for in 1939 came those words spoken on a still September morning "We are now at war with Germany".

My brother and two sisters had been evacuated the week before and only Mum, Dad and I were left at No.11 Childebert Road. The image the three of us made in that kitchen that morning, listening to those words of Neville Chamberlain will never leave me. Neither will that feeling of dread those words brought to us. The unthinkable had happened. "We are now at war with Germany". This was the first time I had experienced a terrible fear. A fear that came from the core of my being. An inherited fear, not one born of one's own experience. It was as though part of an ancestral memory had been awakened and brought a kind of dread I will never forget. But, then who of us who heard that Sunday announcement will ever forget where we were, and how we all felt on that Sunday morning, 3rd September 1939.

The First World War was not far behind us; the cinema newsreels had covered the bombing of Spanish cities. We had all seen how the history of warfare had moved on. War would not be fought by men in trenches, it would now come to our towns and cities, and to us in our homes. Then, quite unbelievably, the air raid siren sounded. We were to hear it so many times as the war years went by, but on that morning, so soon after Chamberlain's announcement, it had a deadly chill of its own, and our hearts turned right over.

We went out of the front door, down to the front gate, and it seemed that everyone else in the road had done the same. We all looked up to the small amount of sky we could see between the rooftops and we waited. We, who had in the past merely nodded to each other, the men who had tipped their bowlers and said brief "Good mornings," "Good afternoons" and "Good evenings" whenever we passed one another on the road, suddenly became a band of brothers. We talked to each other and we waited. We waited for the sound of aircraft. We waited for the sight of German bombers, and the sound of bombs exploding. We waited. Nothing happened. It was a false alarm.

Though we did not know it then, this was a prelude, an overture to the changes that were coming to Balham. It was the end of an era. It must be hard to imagine, now that we have entered another century, that once Balham had an air of graciousness about it. Even Childebert Road, the lesser of the many roads of grander houses built by Arthur Heaver, had a quiet dignity which would be hard to find today. In 1939, Balham was still in the throes of enjoying a peaceful, dignified, virtually car-free existence and I suppose it was the removal of all our wrought iron gates and railings for the war effort that began the great changes stemming from the declaration of war in 1939. Arthur Heaver's model estates would never look the

Barbara, myself, Megan and Mum,
This photograph was taken by Dad during the early years of the war

same again. In fact the removal of those gates and railings heralded a long slow death to the vision Arthur Heaver must have had when he surveyed over one hundred acres of Balham farmland in 1888 and visualised his finest London estate, with its tree lined roads and houses of character and distinction. But as Dad would say "Nothing ever stays the same, and time moves on".

The Evacuation

In the early months of 1939, the Government had considered the very strong likelihood of German bombing raids should the impending war between Great Britain and Germany break out. Knowing full well how ill-equipped we were to deal with this eventuality they began to look at the way and means of saving the more vulnerable people of London, especially the school children. Plans for their mass evacuation from London began to be considered.

A register was set up for those parents who would consent to see their children go out of London to places of safety in the countryside. Their decisions were spurred on by the very real fear of what modern warfare with aircraft would bring. Thousands signed the registers.

Those who lived in the countryside in small villages and towns were visited by a billeting officer, who assessed the availability of rooms and beds in their homes to accommodate the evacuees from London. One double bed would sleep three children. Only in very dire circumstances were they made exempt from receiving evacuees into their lives and into their homes for the duration of the war and no one believed that it would be 'over by Christmas'.

Megan, Tony, Mum and Barbara on one of our weekend visits to Three Bridges.

In most of the schools in South West London, the evacuation did not start until after the declaration of war. Ravenstone school was among those where the evacuation took place the week before 3rd of September 1939. In the case of Ravenstone school, a set of items had previously been packed by parents for each child and forwarded in advance to the allotted place of safety, and this was to be to a small railway town in West Sussex called Three Bridges.

A pattern was set for all schools to follow. On the day of their evacuation, with the aid of teachers and other helpers, children were assembled in school playgrounds. Labels with names and home addresses were attached to blazers and jackets, gas mask boxes were checked. Then long lines of children would set off for the nearest station. This was happening all over London during the days just before and after the 3rd of September. For most children this was an adventure. For some, a train ride into the country was an unknown treat. There was a general feeling that this was all rather like a Sunday School treat, and soon they would all be coming home again. For the parents who watched their children depart for an unknown destination, most believed that an invasion by Germany was unlikely, but the possibility of air raids was an unknown and unimaginable horror that could happen any day and at any hour.

Going on the principle of 'If we go, we go together' there were those who would not let their children leave. They braved the censure of the Government, their friends and neighbours, and kept their children at home. Ravenstone School kept its doors open for a limited number of hours each school day for the education of the unevacuated, who must have found the Balham roads and the Common very forlorn and silent.

As the days of the 'phoney war' went by, people felt justified in keeping their children at home as they watched the steady trickle of youngsters returning to London. Some came back with their parent's consent. The more adventurous returned unannounced by whatever means they could. Being evacuated in many cases was not a desirable situation to be in. Being alone, unloved and unwanted in an unfamiliar countryside was very hard to endure. In some cases children found themselves being blatantly exploited. Farmers found themselves with extra field workers, and housewives discovered that they had kitchen maids.

There were so many different facets to this world of the evacuee. Some children who had come from very poor homes found themselves, for the first time in their lives being loved and cared for, vermin free, better housed and better fed. These stories and experiences are now fading from our history, but for my two sisters Megan and Barbara (Tony is no longer with us) their wartime experiences as London evacuees will be with them always. The evacuation of the London schoolchildren was a huge undertaking. Nothing like it had ever happened before and is unlikely to happen again, for who, in this world we are now living in today, would stand and watch their children leaving their school playgrounds for an unknown destination, and into the homes of complete strangers?

For some time before I joined the ATS (Auxiliary Territorial Service), now better known as the Women's Royal Army Corps, Mum, Dad and I would board the train at Balham station and head as often as possible at weekends towards Sussex. Megan, Barbara and Tony had been evacuated to the small village of Three Bridges. Whilst there, we would meet and talk to the people who opened their homes to the children of Ravenstone school and walk around the countryside. For just a very short while at weekends, we were a family of six again. Later, there was talk of the children coming home for Christmas. It was a very sad time for us all, and one could not help but secretly wonder if we would be around at Christmas. The future had become a very nebulous thing.

The Blitz

I had the top bedroom at No.11 and after the air raids would boast that I had slept through them all. In fact I lay listening to the steady intermittent characteristic drone of the German bomber. At first I assumed that one lone German plane had circled the house all night, but soon learned that what I was actually hearing was an endless stream of enemy aircraft going to and returning from their targets.

Eventually, I was forced from the top bedroom, which being directly under the roof was vulnerable to the incendiary bombs that rained down on us night after night. My poor mother, who seemed to spend most of her nights dashing about with a stirrup pump, as she had become an ARP (Air Raid Precautions) warden, was frantic with worry, and that only increased what must have been my maddening nonchalance. Dad was forced to put his foot down, and my charade of sleeping through the air raids at the top of the house was over.

Mum cleared a space in the coal cellar, which ran under the passage and front door. Outside to the left of the front door was a wrought iron manhole cover where the coal was tipped down into the cellar. This shaft was to serve as our escape route if the house was hit. Mum, Dad and I, if Dad was not on duty with the Balham Home Guard, slept in the coal cellar. In the blackness of the cellar, we were woken in the mornings to the sound of a large alarm clock placed on a shelf above my head. It would dance madly about as the bell rang and there was always the danger that it would eventually teeter off the edge, so I always had to be very quick on waking to stop it falling on my face.

Looking back to those days, I realise now what a boon those coal cellars were. Based below ground, under the house they were the safest places to be during the air raids. Most of the houses in Balham had cellars and some, like ours, could only have given limited space, but they could not have been so damp and depressing as an Anderson shelter dug into the back garden. Air raid wardens kept lists of people using their cellars, so that in case of massive bombing they would know to clear the rubble and help them make their exit through the coal chute in the front garden.

Those nights in the cellar are ones that I will always remember. We shared our cellar with a pile of coal and many dust-laden cobwebs. It was rather like sleeping down a coal mine, with the acrid smell of the coal, and with electricity in its infancy candles were our only light. But Dad, with his never-ending sense of humour, made those nights bearable. By the time our alarm had gone off, the 'All Clear' had sounded. The Germans had left our skies and were landing their planes across the Channel, whilst we would be patiently waiting for the kettle as it struggled to boil over the merest glimmer of a gas flame. The pressure was always very low after the air raids while our giant gasometers built themselves up again.

One evening in 1940, Mum and I went to the Balham Palladium to see a film. The air raid siren was sounded, but, as the film was nearly over we stayed on to the end. It was very quiet outside, no sound of aircraft, and no gunfire, just searchlights traversing an empty sky. We set off for home, just minutes away, and found ourselves confronted by an air raid warden, who refused to let us continue on home, and insisted on herding us into a brick built air raid shelter, erected above ground, with only the comfort of a reinforced concrete roof. This was outside the cinema in Oakmead Road. Inside the shelter the walls were lined with wooden forms, along with the rank smell of damp old fag ends, and other smells it was better not to identify. Air raid wardens had a lot of power and this one exercised his to the full. No one was allowed to leave that dreadful place until the 'All Clear' had sounded. It was truly one of the longest and most uncomfortable nights we had ever spent and as it happened for our part of London, one of the most peaceful nights of the London Blitz. It was long after dawn when the 'All Clear' sounded and Mum and I together with all the other cinema goers who had fallen prey to the air raid warden's power, were allowed to leave. By comparison the inky black coal cellar at No.11 seemed like a luxurious haven.

Fortunately, wireless reception was generally quite clear in the mornings so that at least we could listen to the well-loved songs of the day as we waited for the kettle to boil and got ourselves ready for the day ahead. If Dad had been on Home Guard duty, he would come clumping home at about this time for his breakfast: Crawford's Crackers and marmalade, if there were any, and tea. After a quick shave, he would set off down the road to open the shop in Balham High Road. He had offered his services to the country by attempting to join up at the age of forty-six but that age was against him. He had to be content with keeping the shop and printing works going, while his partner Mr Mushens, worked at the Foreign Office. He had been drafted there for the duration of the war, where, we were to learn later, he had spent his time decoding secret messages.

Dad's printing business slowed down as the war got under way. Paper became scarce and supplies for the shop dwindled. Consequently, instead of the usual stationary items, he found himself selling luminous walking sticks for the blackout, and a range of other items relevant to the times such as gas mask cases, some cone-shaped, and others simple boxes which were worn slung from the shoulder. These hung in bunches just inside the door of the shop. Reading became even more of a national pastime than ever before. Long spells of activity while various posts were manned night and day found people on duty reading book after book. Evening wireless broadcasts were disrupted with the crackling of static when the air raids started, so that reluctantly people had to turn off their favourite programmes (ITMA- *Its That Man Again*) with the wonderful Tommy Handley, and all the catch phrases that followed like 'Can I do you now sir?' and 'Mind my bike'.

The Balham Home Guard. Dad is sitting fourth from the left.

We eagerly waited all day for Arthur Askey's *Bandwagon* and we were lucky if we ever got to hear the introductory music of our favourite radio shows and tended to open a book instead. It was for this reason that Dad invested in some books and started a library in the shop. We were all encouraged, wherever we went, to look out for suitable books to add to the stock. We bought hardbacks, in those days they cost about half-a-crown (30 old pennies), and were loaned out at two pence and three pence a time, which was sufficient to ensure they paid for themselves fairly quickly. Who in those days could resist authors like JB Priestley, Dennis Wheatley and PG Wodehouse. So, as the war went on, the library grew and kept the shop alive.

On more than one evening, Dad and I would stand in the garden and watch the sky glowing red, the different shades changed and wavered across it like the Northern Lights. The last time we had seen anything like this was when the Crystal Palace burned down, but this was worse, much worse. We knew that the London docks were that night's target for the Luftwaffe.

We were encouraged by the Government to grow vegetables. Everywhere we were confronted with posters that appeared on hoardings, buses and trams and advertisements in newspapers urging us to 'Dig for Victory'. Many did, including my Mum. Part of Tooting Bec Common was turned over for allotments, one of which she received a grant to use. Thus began a series of visits to the Common with a wheelbarrow full of gardening tools, which Mum and I would trundle up to the plot. We had been given a section of what had been a football pitch and, as Mum said, 'It was like trying to dig through concrete'. In fact, as gardening was never one of my prime interests, I was not really much help to her. Neither was Dad because apart from being heavily involved with Home Guard duties, his gardening skills and knowledge were on a par with mine, virtually nil.

We watched Tooting Bec common change as large sections were taken over for anti-aircraft gun emplacements behind their sand-bagged barriers and the barrage balloon sites. I always found the barrage balloons fascinating. Riding high up against a blue sky, they shone like silver and in the rays of a setting sun turned crimson. Sometimes they hung low, each a sagging dark grey mass against a background of white clouds. Mum thought that they looked like "a herd of disappointed elephants".

With the best will in the world, and hours of labour on the part of my Mum, I don't think that the allotment yielded a great deal. Balham may once have been fertile corn and farming land that, one hundred years before, stretched as far as the eye could see, but time and the relentless sprawl of London seemed to have taken the heart out of that small patch of land. It made a very feeble attempt to help us fulfil our patriotic duty, despite the many buckets of horse manure that we collected from our obliging tradesmen's horses and deposited on it. It was a very disobliging piece of ground, that allotment on Tooting Bec Common.

Even now in 2008, there are many of us who still remember the nights of the London Blitz, for to have lived through those nights we have been left with indelible memories that have not been erased by time. On December 29th 1940, Herbert Mason stood on the roof of the Daily Mail building and took his famous photograph of St Paul's Cathedral, ringed by fire on one of the worst nights of the Blitz. Perhaps as he stood there he might have wondered as he surveyed the vista of our burning city, only equalled once before in our history nearly three hundred years ago, was this the end of England and a way of life as we knew it? Because without hindsight we who were there held this unspoken thought as we picked our way through the rubble of our bombed cities after the 'All Clear' had sounded.

Those were the days when our vision was focused on the 'here and now'. We took each day and night as they came and emerged from our cellars and shelters with the dawn of perhaps, just one more day. The ability to look ahead, even to next week, or to think of Christmas was a luxury none of us thought we would ever know again. We were in a war which seemed endless and relentless. In 1940 it seemed the Germans had the upper hand. The German Luftwaffe controlled our skies at night with all the force, energy, and arrogance which seemed to us unequalled, and which we seemed unable to combat. During those nights of 1940 we felt that we were there for the taking.

One of the things Dad gave us all was a pride and a sense of being. We were Londoners. He took us to all the great buildings, museums, cathedrals and abbeys, and used to say as we gazed up into ornamented vaulted roofs, "Now, what do you think of that?" as if he was bestowing a great gift upon us, which, in a way, he was. London was our city to be known, loved and cherished, and fought for. Much later, in the years ahead, when we were at Burrows Lea watching the Trooping of the Colour on television, Dad turned to us all and said "Now, where else in the world would you see something like that?" Much was lost in our city, ancient buildings we knew and treasured, but when we came through and the war was over I don't think we ever looked again at Nelson at the head of his column, the buildings of Westminster, the Abbey, and all the other surviving landmarks of our city without a sense of wonder that they, like us, had survived those long and dreadful nights of the London Blitz.

Dad continued his life, which involved his work at the shop, Essential Services. Most of his nights and weekends were spent with the Home Guard, but interwoven with these was the continuing work he was doing as a healer. Letters were arriving at No 11 in packs. People were braving the 'blackout' to travel across London and from other long distances to see Dad, sometimes bringing relatives with them to meet the man who could heal.

Mum and I spent most of the nights of the Blitz together in the kitchen of No.11, alone if Dad were on duty with the Home Guard, where we would read or knit. And putting off the time

The Balham underground disaster showing a bus that was driven into the crater.

when we would have to descend the steps to the cellar. Knitting and reading was all we could do, and knitting lost a lot of its appeal, because wool was on coupons, and we spent a lot of time unravelling previously knitted garments and rewinding wool to be used again. I felt very deprived not being able to listen to Geraldo or Jack Payne on the Light programme at 9 o'clock or to any other dance band music, especially that of Joe Loss with his wonderful rendition of *In The Mood* which he used as his signature tune.

So we just knitted or tried to read with the noise of enemy planes overhead, and the sound of the anti-aircraft guns, which seemed to be sited all around us, and occasionally the crump of bombs falling nearby. "Where was that?" we would ask each other and exclaim, "That was a near one" or "Someone's caught a packet". When bombs fell nearby Mum, would bunch herself up clutching her knitting and would say "My God, where was that?" I would be terribly calm while pretending to read and reply "It's all right, don't worry, it was only a gun". This was the general pattern of our evenings during the London Blitz. We, with the rest of London, just sat it out.

It was on one of these evenings that we underwent one of the heaviest raids of the war. This was the night of October 14th 1940. South London and Balham caught the worst of the bombing. Mum and I had settled to our evening routine listening to the almighty racket of German planes overhead and the 'Ack Ack' guns all around us keeping up their constant barrage. At about 8 o'clock there was a huge great 'clump' and the house seemed to rise up and fall back, our chairs with it. Before I could speak Mum said "Now, don't tell me that was a gun."

Unknown to us then, one of the worst of the wartime bomb disasters hit Balham. That bomb, when it exploded in Balham High Road, blew a hole through the roof of the northbound platform of the Balham Underground where about six hundred people had gone for shelter from the air raids. Sixty-four people died and many more were injured. The bomb fractured a sewer and severed gas and water mains. For weeks to come Balham Underground was flooded. Above ground a bus and its crew had driven into the crater.

One of the most indelible memories left on me by the London Blitz is of the underground stations being used as air raid shelters. The exodus from the London streets down to the tube began early. Mums with babies, bedding, food and with the children who were not evacuated, made their way down to the underground platforms as early as 3 o'clock in the afternoons to claim their pitch and to hold it for the rest of the working family. By early evening people packed the platforms from end to end with makeshift beds and bedding, leaving just a margin of space for passengers to leave the trains and make their way to the exit.

I will never forget the stench that greeted us when we left the train. It was like encountering a solid wall. As you passed by these densely packed bodies shrouded in blankets, you became aware of the stares as you passed them by, as though you were intruding into their grossly unattractive world. On leaving the train no one lingered, we made for the exit without breathing if we could, and ran for the escalators which would take us up to the relatively crystal clear air of Balham High Road.

Colin Perry, in his book *Boy in the Blitz* recalls much the same when he writes "I squeezed my way on to the train at last and was jammed in, By God it stank like hell of sweating bodies and body odour. Every single station down the line was filled with these refugees from the Luftwaffe... thank goodness I escaped that tunnel of disease. I can foresee disease will be rife amongst people who shelter this way."

Well there was no escape from the Luftwaffe that night in October, when so many of those sheltering in the Balham Undergound were plunged into a nightmare of darkness and rising water. So many mothers with their babies and children trapped in this unknown terror.

This appalling disaster haunted us for months to come. In my mind the echoes linger still, and for a long time after, when all was back in service again, whenever I found myself standing in the hollow emptiness of the northbound platform of Balham Underground, the horror of that night still seemed to hang there, and perhaps it always will.

I had this photograph taken just before my demobilisation for my Mum and Dad.
When I presented it to them my Dad said "Well you do look a sawny (soft) happ'orth" and my Mum said
"When will you ever learn to stand up straight?"

The Home Front

In 1941 I joined the armed forces and enlisted in the ATS. While I was stationed in Surrey and Berkshire I was able to get home for weekend 'leaves' official and unofficial. Dodging the Military Police, without a legitimate leave pass while passing through Waterloo station had become a national pastime among members of the armed forces. I would go straight to the shop and help Dad with the library which had become quite an extensive business. All the books now bore an Essential Services dust cover, which was placed over the original cover as double protection for the books from all the debris they picked up from the activities of ARP wardens, firefighters and ambulance crews.

Then there were the times when Dad and I would go off with a case of the Jack Webber slides and a projector in the evening, or sometimes it would be to give a demonstration of healing. The audiences for these were always large; the name of Harry Edwards was becoming very familiar. Reports of his healing demonstrations and their remarkable results began to appear in the newspapers along with the war news.

Our wartime food rations would be looked upon today in horror. If we could have been given in the 1940s a vision of our supermarkets after the turn of the century, we would not have been able to believe the vast abundance and variety of food today. Food in those Balham days was simplicity itself. Sugar was weighed up and poured into stiff paper cones. Butter, with the aid of butter pats, was taken from a large block of butter, patted into shape, and weighed. Basic dry goods were in packets and there were tinned goods. There was simplicity and little choice. The Sunday joint could be made to stretch until Tuesday, Wednesday was sausage and mash, Thursday liver and bacon, Friday fish, and on Saturday anything could happen. In our house this was a weekly routine you could set your calendar by, so that for us in wartime Britain, as the months went by, we just had less of everything. It was a matter of scraping the precious few weekly ounces of butter on and off the bread, and resorting to sugarless tea or saccharine. Hoarding food was not an option for most of us as there was no extra money to pay for the extra tins to stack away, if they became available. Some people were too poor to buy their full rations.

As the months went on there were many shortages and people looked to their own back yards and allotments which the Government made available to us, and we began to 'Dig for Victory' on our own allotment. Having a chicken-run in the garden was not unusual. My grandmother, when she had lived at No.11, netted off a small section in our small back garden and ran half a dozen hens. Only a limited allowance of chicken feed was made available and this was only granted when the meagre egg allowance had been given up. I remember, at one time, onions became very scarce. Perhaps we had relied too heavily on the French onion men, who before the war would work the London streets on their bicycles festooned with strings of onions. One day, coming home from the Tooting Bec Common allotment, I found an onion in the road. It was such a wonderful find that I could not believe it was real.

When I joined the ATS in 1941, I left behind me all the trials of rationing, 'Digging for Victory', and endless queuing, not that I had done much of all that, it was rather left to my Mum. For the rest of the war for me at least, army rations were plentiful. When I think of wartime rationing two items persist in my mind, powdered egg and spam. All sorts of helpful recipes were broadcast on the wireless and published in newspapers. Exciting ideas about making omelettes with dried egg but no matter what you did with the stuff, it always tasted of wet cardboard.

There was one major breakthrough on the 'Food Front'. We were told that we could make a very passable Victoria sponge using a tablespoonful of liquid paraffin instead of an ounce of precious margarine, which had almost replaced the butter ration, and it worked beautifully in all baking as a substitute for margarine. It was better not to mention the liquid paraffin to the unsuspecting guest as it was used medically as a sort of laxative, and disappeared very rapidly from the chemist shop shelves as soon as the word got around that it could replace margarine so effectively in cake making.

The British Restaurant began to appear in our streets, factories and schools, and replaced other canteens. They became the Government feeding centres and provided very cheap and filling meals. I remember going to a British Restaurant with Dad in Balham High Road and getting a wonderful dinner of mince and mash for ninepence, but mostly eating out meant fried Spam fritters, and we were all becoming very tired of Spam by the time the war was over. One of the legacies of rationing remains with me. I still shake out the last grain of sugar from the bag, still scrape up every sign of butter from its wrapping, and I do hate wasting food. I think most people my age will tell you the same. It is not just perhaps the legacy of war but those distant memories of those hard years before it. It is said that the past is always with us. Perhaps it is.

Throughout the war, Dad's days were full. He had the shop, the Home Guard, and his healing work. He also had been given a dog called Angela. She was a great dane and was destined to become the mascot of the Balham Home Guard, but under a new name to reflect her new role, she was called Hogarth. Bearing in mind the general shortage of food in the war years, I can't remember how she was fed, but do recall whale meat being on sale without the need of coupons.

Megan, myself and Barbara, taken by dad at No 11 in 1944 on my 21st birthday.

When Dad used to lead the Home Guard down Balham High Road to St Mary's Church on Sunday mornings he would do so with Hogarth proudly at the head of the parade. It was rather unfortunate that she had a weak bladder so as the parade made its way along the High Road, its progress was interrupted by a series of unscheduled stops, often sufficiently long in total to cause the organist at St Mary's to fill in time with extra pieces from his repertoire. Nevertheless Hogarth was a magnificent dog. Dad was very fond of her and many times in the years to come expressed a wish to have another great dane. It is just as well that this wish was never made public: he would have been inundated with them.

Towards the end of the war both my sisters were at home. Megan had won a scholarship and was attending art school in Camberwell. Barbara had cut her evacuation short at Three Bridges by coming home on a penny platform ticket, and squeezing herself through past the ticket collector at Balham station by mixing herself in with a large family group. By 'the skin of her teeth' she was allowed to stay at home. Tony had also won a scholarship but as the only options were to train as a chef, or to become a butcher, he decided to wait out the war in a factory in Clapham. In the spring and early summer of 1944, with the exception of myself serving with the REME in Berkshire, the rest of the family were all back in Childebert Road, facing a new peril.

In the cold light of dawn on Tuesday 13th June 1944 an object, the first of its kind, not yet in the annals of aircraft recognition, flew across the Channel and made its noisy way across Southern England. The sound it made has been likened to a very old motorcycle. When passing over London its engine suddenly cut out, followed by a huge explosion. It fell in Bow, East London, killing six people and seriously injuring thirty. This was the first place to experience the destructive effects of the V1 rocket. The 'flying bomb' had arrived. Things changed rapidly when the 'flying bombs' began to fall on London. No one went to school any more as the teachers could not be responsible for the children with this new form of warfare. I found when I came home on my weekend leaves the constant drone of the flying bombs quite unnerving. The sudden cutting out of the engine and the wait for the inevitable crump somewhere nearby, made me long for the comparative peace and calm of the Berkshire countryside, even if it were tightly packed with Canadian and American troops, tanks and lorries and every type of military vehicle assembling for the invasion of Europe.

On my very last weekend leave at Childebert Road I said to Megan as we listened for the next drone of a flying bomb "How do you stand this?" Megan who was going through a religious phrase replied "We are in Gods hands". I legged it back to camp. It was to be my last stay at No 11 Childebert Road, a "flying bomb" saw to that.

Barbara's story taken from her book

Grandmas Wartime Memories

"Since Megan and I had both been back in Balham, Dad got for us a Morrison shelter to sleep under. Tinker, the cat, would join us there and one night Tinker gave birth to two kittens. We were both very surprised, but Mum wasn't. At this time Mum was engaged on war work in London. Dad would come home lunch-times to check on me. I had badly burnt my arm melting down the last remnants of soap tablets which were kept in a glass jar. I had seen Mum melting them down with very hot water, and then put this soap jelly into the copper. Items like soap were in very short supply. I thought I would do this for her and poured boiling water into the jar. It broke, and boiling water and soap jelly covered my arm.

I could not go to school, because of the 'flying bombs'. Everyone you spoke to who had survived the London Blitz seriously wondered if they would survive the onslaught of the V1s and the V2s. We mostly stayed in our homes, which I did after Mum had left for the city and Megan had gone to her art school in Camberwell. I looked after the cat, kittens and the seven ducks we were keeping in the back garden.

People used to say that you never hear the engine cut out of the flying bomb that is going to hit you. I heard the engine of the rocket, and I did hear it stop. There I was in No 11 getting lunch ready for Dad. It was sausage and mash, rhubarb and custard. The cat and kittens were in a basket beside the hearth. When I heard that engine cut out, I whisked the cat and kittens behind Mum's arm chair. The ducks had all rushed into the outside loo. Then came the rush of the explosion. I was knocked to the floor with a door on top of me. The kitchen was full of soot. The cat and kittens were safe, and the ducks were safe. I had to try and let Dad know what had happened. I tried to phone the shop Streatham 0323, but the flex was in my hand.

Out I went through the front door, which had been blown open, and all the windows in the front of the house had been blown to bits. I gathered up the basket of cat and kittens and went to find Dad. Half way down Childebert Road, I saw him turn the corner. Dad always believed in keeping 'a stiff upper lip' and said "Is my dinner ready?" "Yes" I said, covered in soot. We went indoors and looked around. The debris of our home was everywhere. I had laid the table. I think to pacify me, we sat down to have our lunch as though nothing untoward had happened. We heard the sound of crunching glass and an ARP warden came in to see if anyone was hurt. He saw me covered in soot and Dad, eating our lunch amid the chaos and debris of our kitchen as though everything was quite normal. "Well now I have seen everything" he said. We never did find the saucepan of rhubarb.

Inside the Morrison Shelter. Line drawing by my sister Megan Stone

Later Mum, Megan and Tony came back to our wrecked house. Megan had cycled from The Camberwell School of Art, she had spent all that day in the shelter, as the steady stream of 'flying bombs' that day over London had kept everyone underground. She said she had cycled through a nightmare of damage, and round all the bomb debris and rubble that had not been there when she had left home that morning.

Dad phoned his sister, auntie Lily, and uncle Gerald, who lived in Iver, Buckinghamshire, to see if Megan and I could stay there for the time being They were wonderful to us. They looked after the cat and kittens and made us so welcome. Megan and I loved being there with our cousins Eric and Hugh. We worked on Mr Reeve's farm, picking peas and feeding the calves. I don't know how many weeks went by before Dad came to fetch us, and we found ourselves in our new home, 290 Kingston Road, Stoneleigh, Surrey. 290 was a fairly modern semi. Dad and Tony made a pond at the top of the garden for the ducks, not realising that the garden sloped down to the house. They also made Mum a sunken rose garden, and we were not surprised when it rained and the sunken garden filled with water and ducks.

We had a wonderful Christmas that year 1945. I think those Stoneleigh days were some of the happiest we have known. The war came to an end, and everyone was home again."

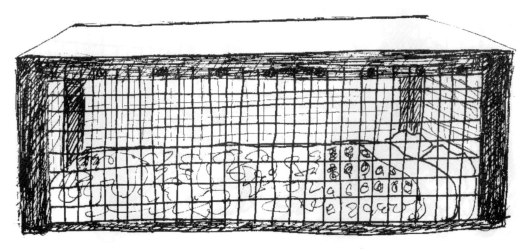

A Morrison Shelter with its reinforced steel roof.
The safest place was the coal cellar, but most people preferred to be above ground.
Line drawing by my sister Megan Stone.

Right: The four of us, having come through the war years. Myself, Tony, Megan and Barbara.

Stoneleigh: Stepping Stone to Burrows Lea

After the 'flying bomb' had so badly damaged our house in Balham, Mum and Dad found a house in Stoneleigh, near Ewell and Epsom, 290 Kingston Road, which was a turning off the well-known Kingston Bypass. So there we were, the six of us, in a new home and a new life ahead of us. Now there was a future in front of us and it stretched away into the years to come. It was heady stuff. The war was over, but memories of No.11 were still in our minds.

The garden in Balham was small and surrounded by fences. It was a square of stony soil which once was part of Hilly Seven Acres, a field belonging to a farm until the late 1880s and must have been fertile corn land, until it lost its soul when Balham became what it is today. Though generally unproductive, it bore flowers that bloomed for Mum. Gardening was in her soul, a gift she passed on to Megan and Barbara, but not to me. I am no gardener, neither was Dad. The only flower he ever seemed to recognise was a hollyhock. They were very common in our London gardens. By contrast with the garden at No.11, the new one in Stoneleigh was large. It is true that the soil was heavy, mostly clay, but nevertheless to my mother, a great joy. Megan, Barbara and I can still remember Dad planting two apple trees there, banging them down, each into a hole filled with water and chunks of ice. They grew!

Perhaps what pleased us all most about our new house was the bathroom. Gone from our lives was the iron bath with clawed feet, which stood at the top of No.11 in a small dark room. Gone were the rainbow discolorations under the taps and our only source of light, a flame of a naked gas jet, which blossomed and flared from a pipe with an upturned end. 290 Kingston Road was just a three-bedroom modern semi, but there we found that we had everything we had ever wanted.

I spent my last leave while still in the Forces in that garden, in the summer of 1945 enclosing election addresses for the Liberal Candidate Squadron Leader Fowler, who was standing as our local candidate in that epic General

Dad revisiting 290 Kingston Road in later years.

Election. Dad chaired most of his meetings. They were to be his last series of public appearances in the Liberal field, his swan song to the cause for which he had worked so long and so diligently since his early youth. It was largely the forces vote which brought in a Labour Government. We who had helped bring about the downfall of Churchill and his Tory Government were jubilant. I remember how stunned the Tory supporters were at this amazing overthrow. But as time went on how many of us did not look back without a feeling of remorse. We had removed a Prime Minister whose determination, fire and grit had propelled us as a nation through the dark war years to final victory. We had a lion of a man to lead us, and if he had not been there we may have been led astray by a string of donkeys. Who knows? What I do know, is that I often look back, and thank whatever powers there might have been for giving us in 1940 the greatest gift this nation could have, Sir Winston Churchill. I can almost hear Dad saying "Amen to that."

In Balham High Road the printing business had picked up after the wartime paper restrictions, and the library continued to attract customers. Dad made his way to the shop every day as usual, though now it was by train from Stoneleigh station. Letters to Dad from patients were beginning to arrive in ever-increasing numbers. Every morning Dad would take a batch of them and once on the train would take a letter from one pocket, read it and transfer it to another. This kept his fellow passengers quite fascinated, while they tried to concentrate on their daily crossword puzzles. In the evenings he took on the role of Healer, to attend to the ever-growing number of people who would arrive at the house for his help.

In those days it was accepted that the act of healing should be accompanied with a sort of pantomime, involving elaborate passes with the hands to the accompaniment of much theatrical flapping and flicking. We had come across some weird exhibitions in our time. Dad, on the other hand, made healing a simple direct act, a reflection of his character for others to emulate. As he was to say so often, and as he once said to my son Steven, "If you want to heal someone powerfully enough just put out your hands and let the power flow through".

Audiences at his healing demonstrations began to grow, demanding a move to substantially larger venues than he was familiar with in the earlier days when we travelled around London in the blackout. Thus, he found himself working in some of the largest Town Halls in the country and detailed accounts of his demonstrations began to appear in the national press. The whole country was beginning to sit up and take notice. Newspaper journalists no longer viewed him with suspicion. The great theatrical journalist Hannan Swaffer, known as the 'Pope of Fleet Street' became Dad's friend, and later was often seen at Burrows Lea.

Dad looked to his family for support, so Barbara left the bank where she had been working in London and she and I dealt with the post which was becoming heavier day by day. I had by then been demobilised from the Army. Dad employed his first secretary, Mrs Shepherd (Kathy), to help with his paperwork and appointments whilst Mum assisted him in the Sanctuary. Only one small room was spared for Dad's healing Sanctuary and patients had to sit on the stairs. In fact they were prepared to sit anywhere whilst they waited as long as there was a chance to see this remarkable man with the power to heal.

With his growing involvement with healing, Dad realised that he would have to give up his daily trips to Balham and began to make plans to pass over Essential Services to his brother, Ernie, who was also a printer and due for demobilisation from the Army. He also realised that he would need more support with the healing itself and one day said to me. "I need your help. If you will come in with me and help me with this new work, I can promise that you will see it grow beyond anything you can imagine." I knew then that my heart would never really be in it, but at that time with Dad under so much pressure, and my demobilisation not so far behind me, and with no fixed plans for my future, I, with my mother, Barbara, and Mrs Shepherd helped him to cope with the mail and the constant flow of visitors to 290 Kingston Road.

I went with Dad to his demonstrations. Sometimes we made very long journeys to the Midlands and beyond. A local man called Mr Hazeldene would drive us to these and during these journeys I would be full of apprehension for Dad. He was not just off to Hyde Park to face a crowd of hecklers: a great deal more was expected of him. He was no conjurer with cards and theatrical props. When he walked on to those now large platforms he seemed to be completely alone and to me, so vulnerable, with only this seemingly very elusive power, which I felt could desert him at any time. I feared for him, but I did not have his inner knowledge. He knew what he was there for and he knew he was not alone.

These demonstrations have been described so many times by the press, and in great detail. We would arrive on the platform and face a sizable audience. Dad would take off his jacket, as he always felt more comfortable working in his shirt sleeves and would ask for people suffering from conditions which could easily be seen to respond to the healing. I have seen a goitre disappear under his hands, leaving only the folds of skin. Dad would unlock arthritic joints, and straighten a spine. People who came up to the platform with the aid of sticks, or with the help of friends, would walk back to their seats unaided. More than one deaf person has heard the ticking of a watch before they left the platform.

As Dad worked away in his shirtsleeves he was surrounded by an almost tangible aura, a field of energy which contained the whole essence of his being, and anyone who has worked with him will understand what I mean. People who came to the platform would normally sit directly in front of him and he, with that wonderful smile, would hold their hands. You could almost feel the vitality and strength that was his, passing to them. When he asked his patients, as he usually did, "What is worrying you? Tell me about it," I could feel that lifting of the spirit that many know so well.

Later, after we had left Stoneleigh, Dad held a public healing demonstration in King's Hall at Belle Vue in Manchester, when 6,000 people came to witness the healing powers of the now well-known healer at work. One of the press reports ran as follows:

THE WORLD'S LARGEST HEALING DEMONSTRATION

Over 6,000 see Harry Edwards at Manchester.

'Before an audience of over 6,000 people, with newsreel cameras making a pictorial record of what took place, and with a greater number of national press men and photographers present than on any comparable occasion, Harry Edwards gave the world's largest demonstration of psychic healing last Friday at Belle Vue, Manchester. The aisles were crowded with stretcher cases and bath chair patients. Mothers clustered round the platform with children in their arms, waiting for Edwards to begin. And it was on healing the children that Edwards concentrated'.

One of the patients that evening was a child called Marilyn Power. The report continues:

'Marilyn Power of Leigh, five years of age and suffering from paralysis of the legs as the result of a recent infantile paralysis epidemic was the first to be treated. The left leg was the worst affected'.

'She had been under treatment at the orthopaedic hospital, Biddulph, for some six months. The child was wearing callipers'.

"Can she walk without these?" asked Edwards. "No" said the mother.

'The callipers were removed. Edward's deft fingers moved up and down the child's legs. Finally he asked her to stand. She did so. Assisted by Edwards, she walked across the platform, then back again'.

Dad treating a spinal condition.

Then she walked down the steps to the floor of the hall still assisted by Edwards. The child had not previously been able to walk down any steps since being afflicted. But, still refusing to wear her callipers, Marilyn at the conclusion of the meeting walked up the aisle assisted by her mother

Further on the report states. 'At this juncture, as mothers were crowding to the front of the platform with yet more children in their arms, Edwards asked whether he should continue with the children or to treat other cases. For the next hour he continued to treat the children.

Cases of blindness and of goitre too were treated, and one patient suffering from goitre shouted into the microphone: "It's gone!" and ran down the steps overjoyed.

Long after the crowds had departed, in a room at the back, unseen by the thousands who were there earlier, Edwards treated the stretcher and Bath chair cases and, true to his promise, saw the children he had been unable to see during the actual demonstration'.

This was not unusual, after every demonstration there would be people lingering after the meeting had been brought to a close and Dad would go down onto the floor of the hall and continue healing for another hour or more. The extraordinary thing about Dad was, after such a demanding demonstration such as he had given in Manchester, and the continuation of healing afterwards, one would have expected him to show some signs of exhaustion, he didn't give any indication of this. In fact, he seemed to be as full of energy and life as before, almost as if a residue of the great power that had flowed through his hands was with him still. Far from being tired, he was in fact even jubilant in the knowledge that he had been the instrument for so much good, that he had left behind him hope, confidence and a belief that 'something' way beyond our understanding, had

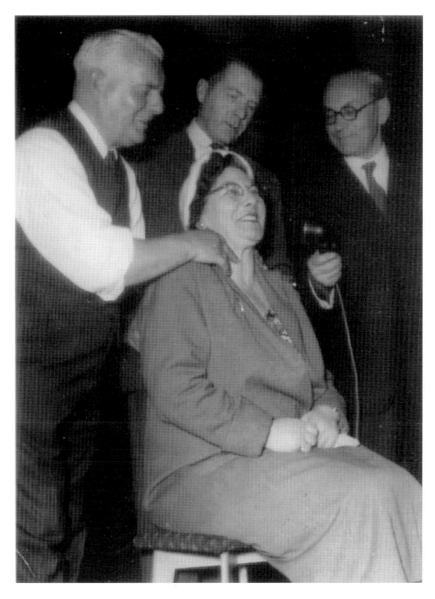

This is one of the joyous moments, and we have seen so many of them,
when the pain has disappeared and the cause is removed.
On the far right is Maurice Barbanell, the editor of Psychic News.

manifested itself and had brought easement from pain and suffering and perhaps for some without hope or belief, a light had been turned on.

It was now 1946. Our short and happy interlude at 290 Kingston Road was coming to an end. It was time to move on to somewhere larger to accommodate the office work and the ever-growing number of patients. We were going to say 'goodbye' to a way of life that we had taken for granted. We believed that our complete safe family unit was indestructible and ours forever. The first real signs of George Daisley's prophesy, that the family would see great changes, slowly came into being. The beginning of this was when we took our first holiday after the war to the Isle of Wight. Our brother Tony was still doing his National Service at this time.

For me it was good to be back on the Isle of Wight. I still had so many good memories after my school journey there earlier, especially of the many journeys we had taken by train across the network of Island stations most of which in summer looked like extensions of the stationmaster's garden. We stayed in a hotel in Ventnor, the Metropole, which faced the sea. My sisters and I thought we were in heaven.

Before we left for the Island, Dad had been approached by relatives of the Governor of Guernsey who was suffering from a terminal cancer. They asked if he would make the journey to the Channel Islands. But in the aftermath of such a recent war, such journeys were difficult to make. However the Governor's son being a staff officer at the War Office, moved in high places and was able to arrange a special military charter flight to Guernsey to take Dad there and bring him back. Weather conditions were not favourable and the flight was cancelled. Another week passed, by which time we were in Ventnor.

The cancer suffered by the Governor was very deep-seated and was causing a great deal of pain and distress, so another attempt was made to get Dad over to see him. We had not been on our holiday for more than two days when a military representative came to our hotel to ask Dad if he was prepared to travel to Guernsey right away. He was then driven at speed across the Island to Cowes, and then to the ferry leaving for Southampton. The ferry had been delayed in order for Dad to reach Southampton on time. Later when he returned to Ventnor, he described to us how he was not the most popular person travelling on that ferry. The delay in sailing had annoyed most of his fellow passengers and he found himself being stared at in a very unfriendly fashion. When Dad reached Southampton he was taken aboard a Royal Naval corvette which immediately put to sea and on arriving in Guernsey found the Governor at his residence facing his last days which like the nights and days that had gone before were expected to be long and difficult with so little sleep caused by the endless pain. Dad sat and held the Governor's hands throughout that evening, and the Governor slept peacefully through the night. He lived for a short while longer, just a matter of days. But he had no more pain and there was no need for any more drugs. This surprised his medical supervisors, as they expected the illness to run its course in the way it had before Dad arrived.

While we were in Ventnor, Dad gave a healing demonstration in the local Spiritualist church to which we all went. After that people came to the hotel, and he saw every one. Life was indeed changing. Oddly enough, I returned to Ventnor Spiritualist Church a few years ago, as I was taking a small part in their Open Day by giving a talk on my father and his work. To assist me, my son Mark who, like his grandfather is a printer, enlarged for me a number of significant photographs. These photographs were a great visual aid, and I am sure that Dad would have been very impressed, and very interested in the process which produced such clear enlargements. Of course, this return to Ventnor Spiritualist Church brought back so many memories of that last holiday, and brought Dad back so closely. In fact it was nice to hear from one or two people at this meeting telling me that I was not standing there alone, which did remind me of Dad one day saying "Remember, after my passing I will never be far away. My work will still continue here while I work through others". So on that afternoon it was almost a case of putting out my hand and touching him. I am sure that it would have pleased him to know that I donated several of the enlarged photographs to Ventnor Church.

Just as Barbara said, the Stoneleigh days were the happiest days, but they were coming to an end. We had to begin house hunting. When we returned to Kingston Road there was a letter from the Governor's wife waiting for Dad. In it she had written "After you left us, it was as though an angel had come and spread his wings over my husband. He had no more pain".

The Perfect Place

In the summer of 1946, the war being over, there were many large houses for sale which had been requisitioned by various Ministries that had been evacuated from London or occupied by the armed forces, which were being handed back to their original owners. The houses were usually left much the worse for wear and the Government made substantial sums available for them to be brought back into good repair. A large staff was also needed to run them, but gone were the days when one could employ a live-in Irish maid for a few bob a week. After their houses had been taken over, many of the owners had settled themselves in the Dower House, or an estate cottage, for the duration of the war and when it was over were quite happy to stay there. Under these circumstances, the main house was put on the market at a relatively low price.

It was agreed that Dad's sister Ivy and her second husband Alfred Braisier (Frank Pool had died in 1940) who lived nearby us in Ewell would assist Dad in his work. As part of that agreement it was decided that Ivy and Alfred and my parents would sell their respective houses in Stoneleigh and Ewell to provide sufficient funds to facilitate the purchase of a larger property, one of the derequisitioned houses, capable of housing all the needs of Dad's growing activities on the healing front.

We found 'Wood Dene' in Oxshott. It was a large house that the army had used and left in a rather battered state. On every door there was a familiar sign Sgts. Mess, the Orderly Room, the Officers' Ante Room, the CO's Office etc. I felt very much at home in Wood Dene. There were a lot of complications involving requisitioning orders and War Damage claims when purchasing such a house, but we regarded Wood Dene as ours. Ivy and I went to Oxshott day after day. We picked pounds of white, red and black currants, which hung in abundance from the long-neglected bushes in the kitchen garden, combined our sugar rations along with the extra sugar ration we were allowed for jam making and turned the fruit into many pots of jam. Ivy, another dedicated gardener, attempted to clear some of the overgrown flower beds and in doing so exposed a sunken rose garden complete with a statue of Aphrodite.

Strangely, this garden had a very peculiar atmosphere that both Ivy and I were very much aware of, and we both decided that something rather nasty had happened there. But this was of no consequence because it turned out that Wood Dene was not for us. The purchase, so it would appear, could go on for weeks, perhaps months, so the search for a larger home went on.

On Monday 22nd of July 1946, my mother, Ivy and Alfred, accompanied by Ivy's son Alan, on leave from the Navy, came back from one of their house hunting tours of Surrey with the news that they had found "the perfect place". It was outside Guildford and near a village called Shere. The next day my mother and father looked it over and agreed with Ivy and Alfred that it was indeed 'the perfect place', and three days later we all went to see Burrows Lea. I remember that evening so well. We were all sitting in the library with Mr Manesseh the owner.

"You are asking £11,000 for this property?" said Dad.
"Yes" said Mr Manesseh.
"I can only offer you £8,000" said Dad.
"Done" said Mr Manasseh.

Burrows Lea as we first saw it in 1946.

A characteristic photograph of Dad, complete with cigarette, talking to his patients in the sun lounge at Burrows Lea.

That is how Burrows Lea, which was indeed a large house, with some thirteen acres of grounds came to be ours. The sale went through and we all moved in on Saturday 14th September 1946. This was a huge undertaking for my parents and for Ivy and Alfred. £8,000 was a vast amount of money in 1946, and only with the help of a mortgage could it be managed. It exhausted the financial resources of both parties. It was a fearsome thing to do, but we felt this wonderful place coming forward to meet us, as if it too, knew that it was all meant to be.

Burrows Lea had in its past been the home of General Gough who had served in the First World War. Then at some point we were told, an unknown (to us) sculptor had lived there and had used what we called the "games room" his studio, one large lofty room with very wide doors through which his blocks of marble were delivered. Up an enclosed spiral staircase we could walk onto a balcony from which the sculptor would have viewed his work, some of this lay abandoned still in parts of the garden. When we took over Burrows Lea they were retrieved and put on display in the conservatory.

The "games room" became the place to play badminton. Dad was very good at standing on one spot, sending his opponent (mostly me) dashing from one side of the opposite court to the other where he cleverly aimed his shuttlecock, and he was the one who was supposed to be losing weight! Now, sadly, the lofty games room is no more. It has been put to a more practical use. I say "sadly" as a deep sadness is what I felt when I last saw it in its new form. Perhaps that is because I was standing with the ghosts of former days and wishing so much I could go back and be with them all again, especially to be there with my Dad and his very clever standing on one spot badminton game.

Mum used to hold her Old Time dances in the games room, and it was ideal for her amateur dramatics. Before we took over Burrows Lea, the games room had been requisitioned and the woodlands around it by the Canadians and a transport unit had been stationed there during those vital months before the invasion of France. The only signs left by our Canadian visitors were deep tracks left in the woodland by their heavy vehicles. Burrows Lea had also been home to the Colmans Mustard family.

Dad in the Burrows Lea Conservatory admiring the work of the sculptor who had been in residence at Burrows Lea at one time.

Once we had established ourselves at Burrows Lea we looked for the staff to help us run the place as a healing Sanctuary. One of the first people on the scene was the wonderful Phyllis Harding who ran the main office until she retired many years later. Dad thought so highly of her throughout the years they worked together. By now the mail was arriving by the sackload and local ladies who worked from their homes were typing his replies. At lunchtimes Dad would sit with a mountain of typed letters before him and sign each one. He refused to have a stamp with his signature made, and this routine went on for years.

Before we left Stoneleigh two helpers had arrived to join Dad. They were both healers, Bill and Dolly Brown. However by the time the Stoneleigh days were over Bill and Dolly had decided to leave for a new life in Australia, so after their departure it was left to Mum and I to assist in the Sanctuary or to help Barbara with the endless pouring of afternoon tea for the coachloads of patients who arrived from Guildford and Dorking North stations. Megan was now attending Guildford Art School. Barbara and I spent our mornings in the office opening and sorting the mail. There were also the evening trips to London and elsewhere when Dad would give his public healing demonstrations He liked us to be with him.

The days were full and very busy and help was needed. It came. Soon there were dedicated people assisting Dad and helping with teas. Along with them came Mrs Nicholson. She was an elderly lady full of energy, kindness and wisdom. She had been the wife of Major General OHL Nicholson who had given valuable service in India during the First World War. Eileen Nicholson had travelled the world with him and had acquired so much knowledge and a great deal of understanding and compassion. I myself have reason to be grateful for her sound advice. Dad and Mrs Nicholson, who he affectionately called 'Peter' came to know each other well and he greatly valued her friendship, as did we all. Eileen Nicholson was a star and not one of Dad's future assistants in later years was able to compete with her light. As I write this, so many years later, I know that light still shines for me, as it must do for those who still remember her.

*In the early days of Burrows Lea, when something miraculous seemed to happen every day,
Eileen Nicholson arrived as a helper in the Sanctuary.
With her came a wealth of wisdom, compassion and a clarity of vision,
which made her presence a very welcoming fact, not only for the family and the patients but especially to Dad.
He valued Eileen Nicholson's friendship very highly, and it is very pleasing to those of us who still love
and remember her to know that there is a healing room at Burrows Lea named after her.*

Soon after we arrived at Burrows Lea Mum had her wish. A house cow arrived, a shorthorn-cross-Guernsey. We called her Honeydew. She was a very much loved and pampered creature. Wartime restrictions were still with us in those early days and the butter that Mum was able to make came in very useful.

Now and again someone in America who was in correspondence with Dad would send us a food parcel. I remember tins of very strange tea arriving, very strong rank-tasting tea; the tea leaves after the tea was made resembled bat's wings. Dad who liked his tea very weak did not like this 'bat wing' variety but the rest of us made do with it. Tony returned from doing his National Service and went into farming.

With the arrival of Mrs Nicholson, I was able to slip away from my duties in the Sanctuary. I knew I had another path to follow, and it led down to Tower Hill Farm in Gomshall where I started my long love affair with the British dairy cow. Eventually I became a student at Merrist Wood, a farming college in Worplesdon, Surrey. It was here that I met my husband, Paul, who was taking a course in horticulture.

Myself and Honeydew, the much loved and pampered housecow
at Burrows Lea.

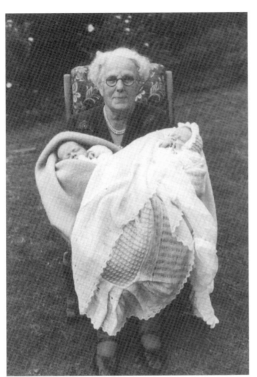

We were married in 1948 and my days at Burrows Lea were over. Paul and I with Megan and her husband Vic (another Merrist Wood student) took up farming in the West Country.

By 1957, Paul, I and our three sons, Steven Mark and Tim, were back in Surrey and not too far from Burrows Lea. We had a glasshouse nursery between Horsham and Guildford. So weekly visits home to Burrows Lea brought me into Dad's orbit again. My fourth son, John, was born in 1960.

At that time Dad was fighting for some recognition from the British Medical Association, and from the Church, but received nothing. The overwhelming evidence he presented to them was either belittled or disregarded. Television companies and sometimes the Press seemed to do everything they could to discredit him. In spite of this he worked unceasingly to raise

Nanny with my son Steven and Megan's daughter Jill at her christening carried out by Dad in the Sanctuary.

It was never difficult to decline taking a cup of tea with Dad. The tea was almost colourless, that is the way he liked it.
Even after so many years have passed since tea was on offer with Dad
the family always refer to very weak tea as 'Burrows Lea tea'.

The christening of Barbara and Alan's second daughter Angela. Megan with her first three children, Sue, John and Jill, Mark myself and Steven, Dad, Barbara with Angela and Sheila.

Dad with two of his grand-daughters Sheila and Angela

This was a familiar sight on Dad's birthday and at Christmas. Cards poured in from all over the world. It was an overwhelming display of the affection people had for our Dad.

public awareness of the healing potential and to encourage others who wished to emulate him, to develop their ability to heal. Moreover as a direct result of his own efforts the National Federation of Spiritual Healers (NFSH) was formed and Dad's sister Dorothy, after her husband's death in 1957, had joined Dad at Burrows Lea and became Secretary of the Federation.

Friday lunchtimes at Burrows Lea became the highlight of our week. Sometimes we were joined by Ray Branch, who was becoming Dad's right-hand man, his humour matching Dad's. Paul, who was an ardent Labour supporter, during election times suffered their banter with equally good humour. During one of the elections that were taking place, he found himself driving away from Burrows Lea with Liberal stickers all over the back of the car, while he supported Labour from the front. I did wonder why Dad and Ray had taken so much trouble to see us off. All through these years of fame at Burrows Lea, Dad remained to us the same man we had known and loved throughout all our years together in that terraced house in Balham. His worldwide success as a healer, and his now quite considerable fame, did nothing to change him, which brings me to one of those moments which endeared him so much to us.

We had important guests from Holland staying at Burrows Lea for the weekend, and Barbara and Ivy had gone to a lot of trouble to lay the table for breakfast. All the signs of the usual Sunday morning breakfast scrummage had gone and the table was beautifully set, everything shining and sparkling; the toast was in thin perfect triangles. We all made a somewhat stilted group around that perfect Sunday morning table until Dad appeared. He stood and surveyed the table for some moments, disappeared into the kitchen and returned a few moments later with a large battered enamel bowl of turkey dripping. Ivy was not too pleased to see this, but for me it brought back a refreshing breath of Balham, of Boxing Days long gone, when a similar chipped and battered enamel bowl of turkey dripping would appear, for Dad to enjoy with his toast.

Life at Burrows Lea continued over the years. It was a time when so many people came and went, some famous, some important; writers, investigators, well-known journalists, even Royalty, not only from this country but from abroad. Then there were the weekend visitors.

There were so many times when sitting with Dad in the garden, we would see visitors coming towards us across the lawn. He had opened up the woodlands and lower walk to the public, and it was never long before they spotted him. Then of course he would invite them into the Sanctuary. Our sunny afternoon with Dad in the garden would be over. No one was ever turned away.

Here stand two printers, one retired and one yet to come.
It is unusual these days to see the old family traditions of following one trade
from generation to generation.
Dad's father was a printer and now Dad's grandson Mark has an established
printing and label business here on the Isle of Wight.
Mark is now in close contact with the charitable trust of Burrows Lea and has
printed this book as well as other projects for the Sanctuary thus maintaining a
link between the family and Burrows Lea.

Dad with his Harrild Press.

Mark operating a Heidelburg Press in the 1970's.

Dad was always very keen on jigsaw puzzles. During our years in Balham, he joined a jigsaw puzzle library. Every Saturday he would turn out some incomprehensible jumble of pieces from a plain box with no indication of what the finished result was to be.

In one that I remember, all the pieces were just shades of pale blue and it eventually became a picture of a pale blue sky meeting a pale blue sea.

There was a bit of a delay in getting this thing started, as Dad had to discover that the edges were a series of small loops and the straight sides were inside the picture.

In later years, he exchanged jigsaw puzzles for painting by numbers, which was a very relaxing occupation and one he seemed to enjoy.

Dad and his sister Dorothy at the healing centre at Loughton.
Some of my paintings on the shelf just behind Dad became part of the annual sale of work.

Oils and Canvas

Though I had not the gift of healing, I did develop the gift I had for painting. This had always been encouraged by Dad. He had made sure that I had a box of Reeve's watercolours in my Christmas stocking throughout the years of my childhood, and later gave me my first oil paints in a large wooden box. One day Mrs Nicholson gave Dad a book called simply *Surrey* illustrated by Sutton Palmer and described by A.R. Hope Moncreiff. Those colour plates of Surrey scenes were my inspiration. It became my goal to paint like Sutton Palmer. I borrowed that book and it never went back to Burrows Lea.

By the time my fiftieth birthday had arrived I was still taking lessons from Robert Root-Young on the Isle of Wight where we moved in 1967. Dad's brother Ernie, having sold the Essential Services shop in Balham in 1968 also moved with his wife Lily and his daughter Rosemary to the Island and lived in the nearby village of Freshwater. Ernie and I shared the same enthusiasm: we loved to paint. So on one of my less frequent visits to Burrows Lea, I was delighted when Dad said "There are several canvasses in the games room. They have been there for some time. If they are any good to you, take them".

It turned out they were mostly relatively large portraits of very unlikely-looking 'spirit guides' and someones vision of the 'Astral Plane', which looked a very lurid place, not somewhere you would wish to go. I joyfully brought most of them back to the Isle of Wight and collected the rest later. To paint on canvas was a rare delight, one that Ernie and I could not easily afford. We set about with our oils and had the time of our lives covering the existing works of art with our own masterpieces.

After lunch during my next visit to Burrows Lea, Dad's sister Dorothy produced a letter and said "I have a letter here from someone asking for the return of some paintings she sent here on loan. She needs them for an exhibition." It did not take me long to realise from her descriptions of the paintings that most of them by that time were submerged under a cover of painted landscapes and Ernie's unusual conception of the Needles Rocks and lighthouse. I mentioned this to Dad. "Are you sure?" he asked. "What can I reply to this woman?" asked Dorothy. We all waited for his answer but he went on with his endless task of signing letters. At last he looked up, smiled at Dorothy and said, "I'm sure you will think of something". I never did find out what that was.

My painting skills had improved under the guidance of Robert Root-Young who held art classes in Newport. I took my efforts home to show Dad. He was quite impressed and asked me to paint some more for him to put in the next 'sale of work' at the National Federation of Spiritual Healers Headquarters in Loughton, Essex. I responded by painting several Daler boards for him. He sold them all. I was elated, but not for long. Ray Branch said "If your father was selling bent hairpins people would buy them" and when I told Robert Root-Young every painting had sold he said "Well, some people will buy anything." In spite of this overwhelming encouragement, I carried on.

Along came 1973, and Dad's eightieth birthday due in May. In April I had a letter from him, saying that members of a Spiritualist church in the north, which had been demolished, had sent

71

him, at great expense, a large painted canvas which they thought he might like to have for his Sanctuary. It was five-and-a-half by four-and-a-half-feet, a very crude painting of Christ healing the sick. It was not exactly what Dad wanted for his Sanctuary, even if it could have supported a canvas that size. "Do you think you could do something with it?" he asked of me. I could not wait to try. I discussed it with Robert Root-Young, who seemed very dubious about the whole idea "Your foreground detail will have to improve if you are going to work on such a large scale," he said. Then the canvas arrived.

On the 11th of May, I pinned the canvas to the sitting room wall and blocked out the original painting with white paint. The next morning I left the washing up, the beds, and the inevitable upheaval of the home when the rest of the family had departed for the day. I ignored it all, which was not difficult for me, and I went into the sitting room where the canvas was waiting for me. I blocked in a composition from the book of Sutton Palmer's paintings. I picked up my brushes and began. After about two hours, I stood back against the far wall and looked at what had taken shape and experienced an overwhelming feeling of exhilaration. For a moment I thought I was going to fall down. In this elated frame of mind I went over the fields to Westfield Cottage, where Ernie and his family lived, to tell him that it was all working out, and this painting we had talked about since Dads letter had arrived, was really going to happen.

It was another case of forthcoming events and shadows, for it was to be another three years before I began to reach the standard of painting shown on the canvas that day.

On the 29th of May it was Dad's eightieth birthday and we all went to Burrows Lea to celebrate. We took with us the finished canvas. It surprised everyone. When Dad and I were on our own looking at the canvas we had one of those moments of closeness and we were both aware of it. I tried to tell him how at times the brush seemed to move and paint on its own, in spite of me. Then he held out his hands towards me and said "You see, the power is there, just let it come through." We were not a very demonstrative family in the physical sense, kissing and hugging was never part of our behaviour. On this occasion I shared something with Dad, between us came something so much more close and without words we both knew it.

The painting went to Loughton, The National Federation of Spiritual Healers headquarters for Spiritual Healing.

The Finale

As the years went on with all Dad's children married and living away from Burrows Lea life continued there in much the same way as it had before. Coaches still arrived at the front door for the afternoon healing sessions, letters still arrived by the sackload, and important people came and went. I made my visits home from the Island as often as possible. They were happy occasions with Dad and his sisters. Lily was living in nearby Gomshall, Ivy and Dorothy were living at Burrows Lea with Nanny, who well into her nineties needed all their tender loving care.

In 1969, on the 1st of January sadly my Mum died while staying with Tony and his wife on their Isle of Wight farm. She had loved and supported Dad through all the difficult years of the Great Depression of the 1920s and 30s, throughout his political career and on to Burrows Lea. She had been a truly wonderful mother to us all.

I would love to have shared with her what was still happening at Burrows Lea, how Dorothy, knowing Dad's love and interest in all living things, one day presented him with some stick insects in a large plastic container. This was placed on top of the television in the corner of the living room. The conditions there seemed to suit the stick insects very well. They multiplied at such a rate that before long the container seemed to seethe with life, an incestuous pulsating mass, which one was always conscious of. It seemed to dominate the room. As time went by, Dad, like the rest of us, began to feel uneasy over the rate at which this family of stick insects was increasing and said to Dorothy "On the lower walk there is a privet hedge that these insects like. It might be a kindness to release them all there". So Dorothy, who trusted her brother's judgements implicitly, did exactly that. She took the container to the lower walk and, as he had suggested, emptied it out on to the privet hedge, which was actually a part of the boundary that divided Burrows Lea and a market garden owned by our next door neighbour and friend, Bob Bates. The following morning not a stick insect could be found. They had all vanished. But as Dad said later when Dorothy had left the room, "It was better than trying to flush them all down the loo".

There were so many occasions when the whole family would be at Burrows Lea, with the exception of Ethel who died just before the war. Dad's remaining five sisters and two brothers would gather there with their families during the summers, and every Christmas. They are the Christmases the like of which Burrows Lea will never see again. For thirty years Burrows Lea was the focal point for the family, the one place where so many could gather together and enjoy the deep bonds that had always united us, the family, and Burrows Lea was part of us.

But then it seemed:

*"The rose of summer was ours forever
Who could have seen those petals fall?"*

For Dad's eightieth birthday the National Federation of Spiritual Healers had booked the Royal Albert Hall for a celebration Healing Demonstration. The family, Dad's brothers and sisters and his children and their families gathered at Burrows Lea for the weekend. This was to be an occasion that we were to remember with love and with great pride. It was almost as though those of us closest to him were to be given a Grand Finale. Time was running out. There were only three-and-a-half years of Dad's life left to us.

On the Sunday evening, coaches arrived to take the family, and by now a very large office staff, plus everyone else connected to Dad and his work, to the Royal Albert Hall in London. Inside that great hall on that late May evening, as I looked around at all the summer dresses and hats, I thought how like it was to a huge flower garden. There was something else too, an atmosphere, an atmosphere created by all these people who had gathered there that night for a man they all loved. It was a tremendous and almost tangible feeling. When Dad walked on to that platform and faced well nigh on five thousand people, they rose as one from their seats and gave him a tumultuous ovation. It went on for a long time. No one, it seemed, wanted to stop. It was a spontaneous and moving act.

During that demonstration the healing just seemed to flow from him. The people that came to the platform responded to the healing. Some of it was quite spectacular. Dad appeared to be in better form than ever before. He even seemed to be younger than those eighty years he carried. He was so much his usual jovial self, and as that wonderful evening went on, I had the impression that the Royal Albert Hall, so vast, had become a small intimate place. It was just like being at a birthday party. I can see now that we, his family and friends, were being given a time to remember, that one might almost say was 'a gift from the Gods'. The blueprint was nearing its final stages. It was time for us all to start saying Goodbye.

Dad left us on the 6th of December 1976. There was no funeral as such for him. I remember us both sitting together on the afternoon of his sister Dorothy's funeral.

"When my time comes" said Dad, "I do not want a funeral or people coming to say 'Goodbye' I am not going anywhere. I will still be here." We did respect Dad's wishes and his lonely coffin made its solitary way to the crematorium.

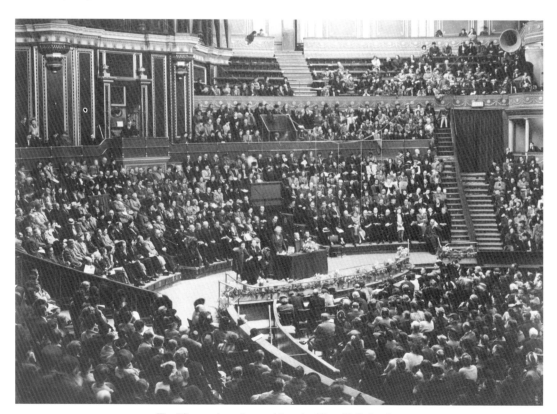

Five Thousand people crowd into the Albert Hall, London.
The occasion was a healing demonstration to mark Dad's eightieth birthday, May 29th 1973.

We the family all gathered at Burrows Lea on that day for the very last time, for now Burrows Lea had passed into the hands of the Trust which Dad had created earlier and was to become the Harry Edwards Healing Sanctuary. We were only there as guests. We were all as sad as the house itself.

A well attended healing demonstration.

Harry Edwards with man's best friend

Hello Dad

In 1983, seven years later, Dad's youngest sister, Marjorie, who had also moved to the Isle of Wight, suggested that we had a 'sitting' at her house, where we rather hoped we might contact Dad. During this sitting I was told that I should "sit and write". Well, I laughed at this as I had not the staying power or the discipline to write. Marjorie then said "I get the feeling that they want you to try automatic writing."

This amused me even more as I was rather sceptical about automatic writing, believing it to be one of the easiest con-tricks in the business. Dad eldest sister, Winnie, was with us at this time and agreed with Marjorie that automatic writing was something I ought to try. Winnie, like my father, was a healer. She had been practising for many years and set up her own healing centre in Streatham, S.W. London. But her approach to healing was very different from Dad's. At Shere, in the peace and serenity of Burrows Lea, Dad had worked in an atmosphere of relaxed calm. Auntie Winnie, on the other hand, had a substantial house in which one large room served both as church and healing centre, that seemed to be forever full of people, cups of tea, and children charging around with great yellow sticky buns.

Auntie Winnie complete with fag, would work away in an atmosphere of noise, clatter and chatter. She had an army of willing helpers; some were also healers, others carried round trays of tea and plates of cakes. There was a lot of laughter, noise and happy chaos all around her which I found quite refreshing, and Auntie Winnie's healing powers, which were quite considerable, seemed happy enough to flow from her regardless of this slap-happy state they found themselves in.

"Why don't you try automatic writing?" she suggested on that particular evening. "It will come, if you let it." So I tried, night after night I tried. I would absent my mind from the pen by reciting poetry and with my eyes closed would feel it moving all over the paper. It just produced aimless scribble. I set the pen simple tasks like asking it to move through the centre of a dot. It failed to do this, though I could feel a form of power passing through my finger to the point of the pen, when it would feel almost alive, so I began to weary of this pointless exercise. Then came the time when I said "Right, that is enough. Five more minutes and I am packing this in." The movement of the pen changed from its meandering across the paper and there was a different motion altogether. I opened my eyes and saw the name "Harry" Not Dad, or Henry, as he was known by in the family, but Harry, his more professional name.

I can't describe what I felt. It was one of those moments of great elation. This experience has been described as a 'magic moment'. I have known many such moments in my days as a painter, but the sight of that name was best of all.

The writing began to change, became more loose, the pen moving easily and the writing began to flow across the page. I still went on reciting all the poems I had ever learned, and at the end of the pen's movements would stop to sort through the lines of rubbish from where I could pick out whole words. The very first message I saw was this:

"I must go landwards, many thoughts away, and calm my mind, and learn where everything is slow, for the days in this other land come warm and long." It sounded like heaven.

As the writing progressed, I was able to tell my son Steven that he was a healer:

"Does he not know that he is a healer" wrote his grandfather, "and that I am always with him?" Steven would never have had the confidence to start healing, which was always something he had wanted to do; without this direct message from his grandfather.

The writing went on in various ways and in the end became more direct when a whole collection of poems were eventually written, but that simple early message for Steven was the one that had to be written, and the one that really mattered.

Steven lives in Wales with his wife Pauline, a very perceptive and sensitive person, who in the early days of his development was able to relay directions to him that she was hearing clairaudiently from Dad. It was quite extraordinary to hear her passing messages to us that she was hearing from Dad. They came across with all his wonderful humour. Pauline had only known Dad briefly before he died, so it was not possible that she was manufacturing them herself.

Once, when I told Pauline I was going to put the kettle on for tea, she said "Your Dad says he will have his under the hollyhocks in the garden" There was no way that Pauline could have known that hollyhocks were one of the few flowers that Dad could name. He was using the word 'garden' to describe the place where we all eventually gather and is probably another name for the 'Astral Plane'. It seems to be a place that links this world with the next.

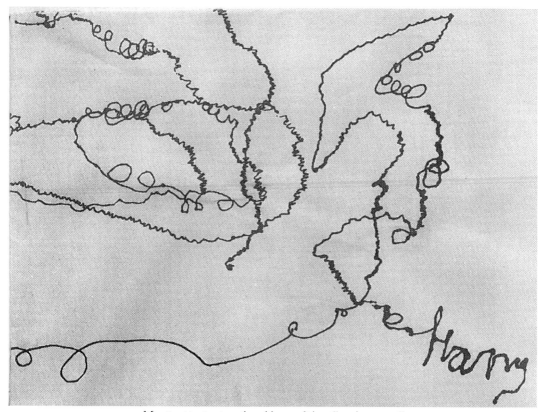

My attempts at automatic writing result in a "magic moment"

I remember a night in a Welsh farmhouse, when Steven was giving healing to a farmer called Graham. He had cancer and had been given six months to live. It was a very homely scene. Two boys were playing draughts at the kitchen table; Anne, Graham's wife, was sewing; Steven and Pauline were standing by the seated Graham. Into that farm kitchen came that almost indescribable sensation that one experienced when Dad was giving one of his demonstrations or working in the Sanctuary at Shere. It was that indefinable something that surrounded him when he was healing, and that kitchen was full of it. I suppose one could say it was filled with his aura. If I had been a clairvoyant, I would have seen Dad in his white coat, sitting before Graham with both hands on Graham's solar plexus. He was there. I knew where he was and what he was doing. That was years ago, in 1984, and Graham is still with us, and it is now 2008.

Shortly after this Steven and Pauline visited the Island. A member of our family had been childless for some years. Pauline said "Your father is here and is saying that he wants you to bring her over here to the Island. He wants to work through Steven. He says that she will have a baby next September. It will be a girl and he wants her to be called Cherry after the Cherry tree walk planted for him at Burrows Lea". Well, I was dumbfounded by this message, and for the life of me could not bring myself to do anything about it for fear that I was asking her to set out on what I thought could be a wild goose chase.

To my shame I decided that I could not think of raising anyone's hopes in this way. Before leaving the Island and returning to Wales, Pauline said "Your Dad is saying don't worry, he will work through Steven in another way". This was in November 1985. The following year a child, a little girl was born, not in September it is true, but on the 2nd of October, which for me was near enough. Sadly she was not called Cherry. It is quite a thought when one considers that the child's birth was foretold so positively two months before the actual conception.

But then, how different was this from all the other incredible happenings that had occurred since the early years of Dad's healing? How many times have we seen him walk into the living room at Burrows Lea with a letter in his hand saying "Do you know what I have here, a letter from a patient who says her doctor and the hospital consultants are baffled. The cancer that showed so positively on previous X-Rays has now completely disappeared?"

I think that Steven, like myself, will recall Dad saying "Always remember this, after my passing I will not be far away. My work will continue here. Just put out your hand and I will be there." Which makes me feel that the blueprint still continues.

I have travelled along through a large part of that blueprint with the rest of the family. We went through the Great Depression of the 1920s and the 1930s when Dad was a printer and a stationer. I watched his gift of speech and his presence as a public speaker develop which, unknown to him, was not to end in Parliament. It was part of another plan to project him forward to places unseen and undreamed of, and the first of these took place in a meeting house in Cloudsdale Road. There was all the excitement and awe as his first healings took place, and then there were the amazing days of Jack Webber, short-lived as they were. They brought so much knowledge and insight revealing the hidden powers that lay beyond us, as yet unexposed and unexploited by man. But as Dad used to say "The time will come when all this will be ours to use". The power to dematerialise, which was clearly demonstrated through Jack Webber's mediumship, may one day be used for man's travel into space. War was declared, and as a family we went through this dark period in our history. Against all the odds piled against this country in the early days of the war, we came through, and all the while Dad's role as a healer was building as his confidence and vision grew.

*Steven and Pauline who carry on the work
of healing in Wales today.*

The time came at Stoneleigh when we were given a short breathing space. The war was over, there was a future for all of us. Dad had reached the peak of his healing powers, and as George Daisley foretold, life was about to change. And change it did.

Each change and sequence in Dad's life had reached its fulfilment. Burrows Lea lay ahead of us, and for Dad it was another threshold which he viewed with all his faith, optimism and confidence, and these he seemed to pass on to his patients as they sat before him in the Sanctuary. I remember a taxi driver telling me how he picked up patients from Guildford station who were making the journey to Burrows Lea, and not knowing who I was said, "I don't know what goes on up there, but when I return to pick the same people up, they are different people. So much more full of life, as if they have been touched by some sort of magic."

The blueprint was set to run through the next thirty years while Dad and Burrows Lea evolved around each other. All his four children married and left home and went their separate ways, but always returning back for family occasions, for Christmas, summer parties, weekends, and holidays, and at the heart of it all there was Dad. Some years ago I visited Burrows Lea when it was being put through all the changes to become the place it is today. I just felt a dreadful sadness that the Burrows Lea I knew and loved was now lost in the past.

When I walked out through that front door for what I thought was the last time, I felt Dad walk through it with me as I was leaving, and I heard his words "Now, you should know by now that nothing ever stays the same. You must put the past behind you. Just let it all go. It's time to move on".

Then I knew he had turned and had walked back into the house.

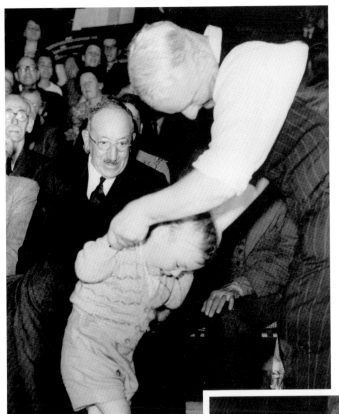

Help being given to a four year old boy to
take his first steps.
Due to a disease of the spine young John
Greeves had never walked before.

Another child is helped to walk.

*This photograph portrays the great bond of
affection between Dad and his mother*

*A public healing demonstration where Dad is accompanied by members of the National Federation of Spiritual Healers.
The Federation was created by Dad who was its' first member.*

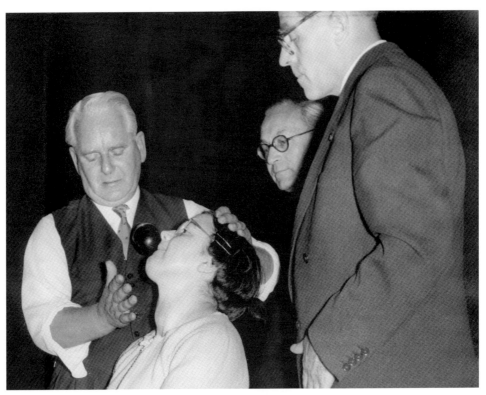

The disappearance of a goitre was a form of healing easily demonstrated at a Public meeting. The visual evidence was there for all to see.

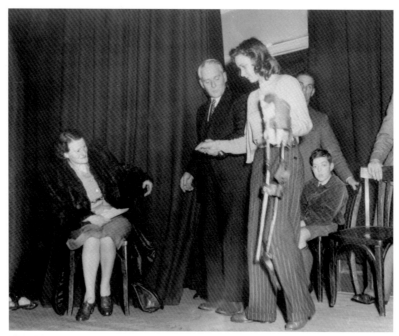

My Mother who accompanied Dad to many of his healing demonstrations, is seen here on the platform with him.

The healing touch.

Here is the photograph most loved by family and friends, how many times have we met that same look across the living room table at Burrows Lea.